U0677610

像美国人一样地道发音

AMERICAN ENGLISH

>>>>>

熊叔 | 著

浙江教育出版社·杭州

图书在版编目（CIP）数据

像美国人一样地道发音 / 熊叔著 . -- 杭州：浙江
教育出版社，2019.11
ISBN 978-7-5536-8278-5

Ⅰ . ①像… Ⅱ . ①熊… Ⅲ . ①英语－发音－美国－自
学参考资料 Ⅳ . ① H311

中国版本图书馆 CIP 数据核字（2018）第 296300 号

像美国人一样地道发音
XIANG MEIGUO REN YIYANG DIDAO FAYIN
熊叔　著

责任编辑：赵清刚
美术编辑：韩　波
封面设计：荆棘设计
版式设计：刘龄蔓
责任校对：马立改
责任印务：时小娟
出版发行：浙江教育出版社
　　　　　杭州市天目山路 40 号　邮编：310013
　　　　　电话：（0571）85170300-80928
　　　　　邮箱：zjjy@zjcb.com 网址：www.zjeph.com
印　　刷：天津旭丰源印刷有限公司
开　　本：880mm×1230mm　1/32
成品尺寸：145mm×210mm
印　　张：10.75
字　　数：221 千
版　　次：2019 年 11 月第 1 版
印　　次：2019 年 11 月第 1 次印刷
标准书号：ISBN 978-7-5536-8278-5
定　　价：45.00 元

版权所有，翻印必究。如有质量问题，请与我发行公司联系调换。

推荐序一

（劳伦斯·布鲁斯之前是上海外语频道的语言顾问、声音总监，曾录制过无数纪录片，获得过上海白玉兰奖。即便没看过他录制的纪录片，他录过的很多四、六级听力材料，应该已被数以千万计的大学生们反复听过。）

It was in 2010 that I first encountered Uncle Bear when working at Shanghai Media Group.

2010 年我任职于上海东方传媒集团有限公司，正是在这一年，我初次与熊叔相遇。

He was an intern at International Channel Shanghai where I was doing voice-over announcements and a little bit of training of anchors.

当时他在上海外语频道实习，我在那里担任解说员，也承担一些训练主持人的工作。

I heard his recording of a short news report and was immediately struck by the quality of his voice. I assumed that he had been educated in America and had taken some voice classes.

在听了他的一小段新闻报道录音之后，我一下子就被他浑厚的嗓音吸引了。我猜他一定在美国留过学，肯定还参加过语音培训班。

Imagine my surprise, then, when I discovered that he was so young and that he had lived all his life in the north of China. He had never been formally trained, but through close listening to overseas broadcasts he had developed an impressive vocal style and fluency in English.

后来我却发现他年纪尚小，而且居然一直都居住在中国北方，你可以想象我当时有多惊讶。虽然他从未接受过正式的发音训练，但是通过精听外国广播节目，他培养了自己出色的声音风格和流利、地道的英文发音。

Such talent is quite rare, and I encouraged Uncle Bear to take advantage of his special gift and to pursue a career in voice.

这样的才能实属罕见，我鼓励熊叔要好好利用自己的天赋，往声音上发展自己的事业。

He has gone from strength to strength, and by careful self-management has developed a professionalism of international calibre.

他变得愈发优秀，通过细致的自我管理，发展出了国际化的专业才能。

And because he is largely self-taught, Uncle Bear can guide you in your own career by offering some invaluable advice.

熊叔的成就大多系自学所得，因而他能够给你提供宝贵的建议，为你事业的成功提供指引。

Lawrence Bruce
Broadcaster/Narrator/Trainer
Teacher of the Alexander Technique

劳伦斯·布鲁斯
广播员、解说员、培训师
亚历山大技巧教师

推荐序二

重新找到学好英语的信心和办法

最初认识熊叔，是先闻其声不见其人。

2016 年年初，有一个人快速火遍了有书书友圈，地道的美式英语、充满磁性的男中音、幽默风趣的小故事，偶尔还会来点英语说唱，他的声音不断在书友圈中流传扩散，一时间几乎成为书友生活中不可或缺的组成部分，我也忍不住想与他见面，"一睹芳容"。

他就是熊叔。

同年 6 月的一个晚上，我终于第一次见到了熊叔，没有太多寒暄，我们犹如老友久别重逢一般开始畅聊，自此我知道了有关熊叔的很多故事，对他也有了越来越深入的了解，最终我们成了生活和工作中的好朋友、好伙伴。

熊叔是一个充满爱心、永远热情澎湃的人，带给很多人做出改变的希望和勇气。

临近大学毕业，本可以选择留在大城市成为一名专业配音师，他却申请到大西北支教。为了和留守儿童拉近距离，激发他们学习英语的兴趣，他扮小丑、学怪叔叔说话、学变戏法、讲有趣的小故事，把孩子们逗得哈哈大笑，同时也琢磨各种有趣并且有效的教学方法。日后他形成了生动有趣的独特教学风格，很大程度上得益于这一段支教的经历。

能够受到众多书友的喜爱，最重要的因素或许正是熊叔发自内心深处的爱心和责任心，以及由此散发的热情，而这一些都不断感染和带动着无数人。

熊叔是一个追求完美的人。图书《从零开始学英语》的研发历时一年多，熊叔中间几乎没有休息日，从内容教研、视频拍摄和语音录制，到后期课件的制作生产，对于每项他都要求精益求精，大家都说已经很好了，他仍然要再完善每一个细节。看似行云流水、信手拈来的授课，其实背后都包含了他大量的、充分的准备。

熊叔是很多人的"福星"，带给他们重新学习英语的勇气，也帮助他们找到了行之有效的学习方法。用他自己的话说就是，"如果我可以做到，那么你也能够做到"。

听着熊叔一口地道的美式英语，你怎么也不会想到他曾经也是不折不扣的"英语学渣"，曾被很多人嘲笑。在用随身听学习英语的时代，从 ABC 开始到单词，再到句子，从自主学习到师从名师 Lawrence Bruce，从模仿到形成自己的风格，熊叔一路成长起来。这样的成果来自熊叔勤奋的刻意练习，更得益于他不断进行经验总结的良好习惯。

本书正是熊叔自己学习成长、支教以及多年英语教学的经验汇集。书的内容从发音最基础的音标开始，到连读、重读、弱读，再到时态表达，所有关于英语发音从入门到精通的关键点都有简单易用的学习方法和应用技巧。

尤为可贵的是，作为一本专业的英语口语专著，本书一样延续了熊叔授课有趣、有料、有用的风格，读起来就像和熊叔对话一样轻松愉快，一点儿都不让人觉得枯燥。

作为熊叔的处女作，本书汇集了熊叔多年的心血和经验，值得每个期待提升英语能力的朋友认真阅读。

雷文涛

有书 CEO

自　序

你在学英语的过程中，是不是常有这样的情况：

有人教你要"读成这样"，于是你就按照他的声音去模仿，但其实你并不知道这个声音是"如何读成这样"的。换句话说，你知道每个音标的具体发音吗？你知道每个音标的口型、舌位是什么样的吗？

比如：

seat 和 sit 读起来有什么区别？

full 和 fool 读起来有什么区别？

是长音和短音的区别吗？ NO！

cycle 和 psycho 读起来又有什么区别？

这样的例子还有很多，如果只是根据听到的声音去判断，是很难区分开的！因为很多发音是我们汉语里没有的，你盲目地去模仿，很容易模仿错！

熊叔累积教授百万余学生，他们不敢开口说英语的原因，归根结底是对自己的发音不自信！

熊叔蒙受国际语言总监 Lawrence Bruce（大学英语四、六级听力考试"御用"配音）指导，耗时三年编撰这本书，将为你揭开所有的发音疑惑，让你从此自信地开口说英语！

　　本书涵盖两大板块：基础音标和拔高训练。在基础音标板块开始之前，熊叔会先为大家讲解发音以及口语训练的技巧和方法，请在正式开始学习之前，务必了解这些方法！

　　◇ 基础音标部分：

　　每个音是怎么发出来的？发每个音时的口型是怎样的？答案全都在这里。零基础的同学或发音有问题的同学一定要重视这个问题！

　　熊叔为每个音标录制了音频讲解，扫描每节上方的二维码来关注公众号，按照要求回复即可听课和跟读！

　　熊叔在音标部分额外配置了发音练习绕口令以及歌曲，甚至还有熊叔原创的 rap 等，使用这些材料，大家不仅可以巩固音标口型，也能为后面的拔高训练做好准备。

　　需要注意的一点是，尽管音标部分配备了音标的"常见字母或字母组合"，但是英语发音并非像法语、西班牙语那样规律，很多词的发音是不规则的，甚至很多字母组合的发音都是不固定的。比如 read 原型的发音和过去分词的发音就不一样。所以，遇到不会读的单词，一定要查词典确认音标！

　　在音标部分学习内容的最后，熊叔为大家专门配置了"易混淆单词发音"的训练章节，让大家彻底吃透音标！

　　◇ 拔高训练部分：

　　连读、弱读等发音技巧看似简单，但实际上是要求学习者有一定的英语基础的。换句话说，如果一个人英语基础不好，那么能把音标、单词读准确就很难得了，若想要获得进一步提升，务必要先提升英语综合能力。虽然本书内容聚焦于大家的发音，但不要忘记，发音只是语言学习中的一个环节。

　　所有的发音训练，不管是基础的音标发音训练，还是拔高的发音练习，都要从慢速开始，尽可能地慢，时刻感受自己口腔、口型的变化。

　　相信通过对这本书的学习，你的发音能够得到极大的改善！也希望这本书能够激发你学习英语的兴趣，并带给你不一样的学习体验！

前　言

为什么大家的发音总是有问题

英语的重要性现在已经不言而喻了，在英语学习中，发音是最基本的门面。在我参加工作之前，就因为英语发音好而获取了很高的收益。比如，我曾经在投简历的时候附上了一段音频，面试官一听，就直接发 offer 了；大学时候因为英语发音标准，总是会有学弟学妹向我"请教"英语问题；在一次演讲比赛上，外教评委听了我的演讲后直接问："So, you're an ABC. That's cheating."上海外语频道前任的语言总监 Lawrence Bruce（就是大家在大学英语四、六级考试时经常听到的那位声音低沉性感的大师）甚至直接建议我："To take advantage of your special gift and to pursue a career in voice."

可以说，良好的发音面貌能大大提升别人对你的第一印象。当然，这里的"别人"如果是面试官、外教等人就更好了。那为什么很多同学的发音总是让人感觉很别扭呢？我来简单总结一下发音水平的级别吧。

第一级，发音水平最差的，别人不知道说话者在说什么；

第二级，别人连蒙带猜，加上说话者的手舞足蹈，大概能知道说话者在说什么，比如部分日本人的蹩脚英文发音；

第三级，别人基本能听明白说话者说的内容，但总是会憋不住想笑；

第四级，别人能明白说话者说的内容，但是发音很明显带着口音，例如带有类似"东北那嘎达"或者"福南那块子"等的地方口音；

第五级，别人能明白说话者说的内容，但是明显能听出来说话者是个没出过国的中国人；

第六级，别人能明白说话者说的内容，但是不看脸也能听出来说话者是个中国人；

第七级，So, you're an ABC. That's cheating. 也就是说别人听说话者讲英文，会误以为这个人是在美国出生、长大的华人。

大家可以根据自己的经验判断一下自己属于哪个级别。至于为什么多数国人的英语发音很别扭，我再来给大家总结一下。

1. 不学音标。很多同学跟我反映过，说小时候根本没学过音标，都是老师怎么读我们就跟着怎么模仿。那如果老师发音有问题的话，结果就比较惨烈了。不学音标的后果是，每个音都不是很清楚怎么发，那单词、句子合在一起能否读对就更是碰运气的事儿了。

2. 不好好学音标。很多不够专业的老师在教音标的时候，是根据母语的发音生搬硬套的。比如，"你看这个'/i/'的发音是不是跟阿姨的'姨'一样啊"，大家说"是啊"，然后"please"就被读成了"铺栗子"的音。很多同学在学音标发音的时候也是对照着母语发音去学的吧？

3. 综合能力不够强。有些同学的音标学得不错，但是整体发音并不标准。大家要了解一点：发音好所反映的不仅仅是发音本身，更反映出你的整个语言水平。试想一下，你刚学完音标，但是单词都不认识几个就去读句子，你有可能读得好吗？所以想发音好，就得有一定的语言基础，否则光练发音，你会心累的。

4. 没有掌握发音技巧。学了音标、有一定的语言基础，发音还是听着有"一股大碴子味儿"，那就是还没有掌握发音技巧。在这种情况下，你非常有必要对自己的发音进行系统的学习与训练，这事儿就交给熊叔和你手上这本书吧！

英语和汉语的发音对比

重要的事情只说一遍：英语和汉语的发音非常不一样，两者之间没有什么可比性。拿汉语做参考学出来的英语一定是中式英语（外国人听了之后要憋不住笑的那种），就好像美国人拿英语做参考学汉语一样，那一口浑厚的美式中文很难让人听了不笑出声来。

英语的发音，讲究音标与音标之间自然地滑过，而汉语都是几个音拼在一起呈"块儿状"发音的。英语中单词与单词之间往往也会有些紧密的连接，甚至会导致一些匪夷所思的口型变化，就是为了音与音之间"自然地滑过"；而对于汉语来说，汉字和汉字之间的连接往往并没有很紧密，甚至当我说"紧密"的时候也完全可以说成"紧——密——"，每个汉字的发音都比较独立。

我们可以把英语的发音比喻成流水。每个意群（后面会具体讲意群）内所有的单词都像流水一样不间断地滑过。而汉语像是一片树林，虽然所有的树都在同一片树林里，但是每棵树也都可以独立存在。

连　读

前文说过，如果拿汉语去做参照，你的英语发音会很不标准。据不完全统计，汉语有几百种方言：

"绳命是入刺的井猜"源于河北方言；

"倒鸭子"是大连话马路牙子的意思；

自称"胡建"的福建，"福蓝"的湖南；

"瞅你咋的"的东北话，"猴赛雷啊"的粤语；

还有 n、l 和 z、zh 不分的"蓝孩纸""铝孩纸"；

……

这些柔软、含蓄的江南吴语和"大碴子味儿"的东北方言或是其他地方方言，一旦跟英语结合，那可真是"破了相"啦！

所以大家要记住：在你学英语发音的时候，忘记你的母语，把英语的发音当成全新的知识去学习、训练。哪怕有些发音听上去和汉语很像，也千万不要被迷惑。

先了解一下我们口腔的构造。嘴唇、上下牙等大家都很熟悉了。舌头的运用是大家说英语的一个难点。因为我们在说汉语的时候，舌头基本上是比较懒的，不怎么喜欢动，尤其是有些南方人甚至不会卷舌。但是说英语的时候就不一样了，舌头要到处乱撞。我建议大家先用舌头舔一遍自己嘴里的各个部位，从上牙开始往后，熟悉一下自己的口腔构造。

有些音需要大家把舌尖放到上牙后面，这个部位叫上齿龈。英语中的 /l/ 发音就是从这儿开始的。有些音，发的时候又需要大家把舌尖向上碰到嘴里的上层构造（上齿龈后面），这个部位叫上颚。

另外，大家需要了解自己的鼻腔。这很简单，感冒擤鼻涕的时候就能感受到鼻腔的构造。其他需要大家了解的还有舌头的舌身中部、舌根后部，以及声带等。大家把手放在喉结的位置，如果你的喉结不明显，也可以看看自己男性朋友的喉结，吃东西时也会动。

熊叔要嘱咐一下大家，了解了我们的口腔构造之后，在学音标的时候，只听声音去模仿是远远不够的。一定要清楚地知道每个音标在发音时舌头的位置、口腔内部各个部位如何互相配合等，做到知其然并知其所以然。

同时，大家在学习过程中，也要有意识地控制好自己的口腔肌肉。我们在说英语时，口腔肌肉是比我们说母语时更紧张的，但是你又不能过于紧张，否则会失去灵活度。没事儿就张张嘴，感受一下自己口腔肌肉的运动吧。

当然，这样干巴巴地做对比，你是不是会感到迷糊？我们先来看几个实例。

关注微信公众号"熊叔英语"，回复"发音练习方法"，获取熊叔本人音频讲解。

实例 1　她新买了一款 LV 的包，LV 不要念成了"哎咯喂"

辅音 /l/

这个音标的发音有两种情况，当它出现在音节的开头或结尾时，发音的规律是不同的。

1. 在音节的开头。我们把舌尖舔到上齿龈，想象一下有粒牛肉渣塞到你门牙缝里了，你想用舌头把它弄出来。然后你的舌头从上齿龈的地方往下抖，其间声带振动，抖的瞬间发出这个音。所以，想把一个音标读标准是需要你清楚地知道口腔内各部位是如何运作的，不是仅靠模仿就可以的。

2. 当 /l/ 出现在音节结尾的时候，舌尖舔在上齿龈发声就可以了，不要往下抖。

辅音 /v/

这个音标在汉语里并没有相似的发音。很多综艺节目里提到 VCR，有些主持人就念成了"胃吸啊"。

这个音标的发音，是需要我们把上齿和下唇在一起摩擦发出来的。所以它也叫唇齿摩擦音。露出你的门牙来，摩擦你的下唇，同时声带振动，然后发音。

实例 2　穿 Prada 的女王，Prada 不是"普 rada"

辅音 /p/

这是一个爆破音，是由气流爆破产生的。闭上嘴，然后让气流突然冲出双唇，产生那么一瞬间的爆破音，就是这个辅音 /p/。

我们中国人在学这类辅音的时候会遇到一个很大的问题，就是发 /p/ 的时候气流不干净，总喜欢在 /p/ 的后面加上尾音。错误的发音我就不做示范了，需要记住的是，发 /p/ 的时候，气流瞬间通过双唇就可以了，不要拖泥带水。

另外要注意，发这类爆破音时，一定要确保有气流冲出口腔。

实例 3　学好咬舌音

辅音 /θ/

这是一个跟汉语发音毫不相近的音。我们一般会把它叫作咬舌音。舌尖放在两齿之间，让气流通过，通过的一瞬间发出的声音就是这个辅音。千万不要去对比我们汉语中的"四"的发音，两者发音完全不一样。

试着说一百遍 three，是不是觉得舌头被咬疼了？

列举以上几个辅音的实例是想告诉大家，在学音标的时候，千万不要只听声音去模仿，这是远远不够的。你需要明确每个音在发出时舌头的具体位置以及这个音是如何发出的，然后再去模仿。如果你学习了很多年英语，发音仍然有问题，那你应该检讨一下自己，音标是不是学得太囫囵吞枣了？所以我会建议你，把音标再好好学一遍。

实例 4　sheet 不是 shit

元音 /iː/ 和 /ɪ/（美式音标 /i/ 和 /ɪ/）

这两个音，很多同学在学的时候就觉得只是长音和短音的区别。其实不然。

所谓的长音、短音都只是相对的，它们最大的区别是口型。

/iː/（美式音标 /i/）发音时嘴唇微微咧开一条缝，舌尖抵下齿，舌头前端铆足了劲儿向上抬，嘴角咧向耳朵，露出微笑，笑出酒窝最好，这就是为什么外国人在拍照的时候喜欢说 cheese。

/ɪ/（美式音标 /I/）发音时嘴唇微张，舌尖抵下齿，舌头前端仍较高。口腔内部的空间大于发 /iː/（美式音标 /i/）时的空间，嘴角也不会露出微笑。比如，seat 和 sit。

像这种音的区别，光靠耳朵听，起初你是听不出区别的，你只有学会它们正确的发声方法，才能真正感受到区别。当你自己能够说出区别了，你也就能听出区别了。

实例 5　元音 /aɪ/（学习双元音的发音技巧）

我们以这个音为例，带领大家学习英语中特有的双元音。双元音由两个单元音组合在一起。或许有人会认为双元音就是将两个单元音接连发出，并没有什么难处。

其实，双元音最难的地方，恰恰在于这两个单元音之间的连接。这个连接讲究的是自然滑动，也就是由第一个口型自然地滑动到第二个口型。这恰恰是中国人最难学会的地方。

鉴于这种情况，我建议大家把每个口型都拖长，拖到

5 ~ 10 秒。想象成给自己的嘴巴做个瑜伽。我们就以 /aɪ/ 为例，发 /a/ 的时候，张大嘴巴，拖长这个发音，然后慢慢地向 /ɪ/ 滑动。整个过程不要有任何间断，尝试用超过 5 秒的时间去完成这样一个口型的转变。

尝试说 hi、five、like。

到这里，大家应该清楚了，虽然它听上去很像"我爱你"的"爱"，但是实际发音相差很大。我们只有知道这个音是如何发出来的，才能够真正练会它，才能真正解决发音的问题。

以上我们通过举例说明了在学音标的过程中该如何去注意发每个音时的口型。哪怕对于有一定基础的同学，我也建议大家重新回顾一下音标的学习，看看自己是不是真正学会了每个音的发音。在本书的音标部分，熊叔针对每个音标都提供了大量的训练素材，从最基础的音标、单词到句子应有尽有，甚至每个音标都配上了绕口令或可以 rap（说唱）出来的原创歌词，尝试用不同的趣味方式帮助大家掌握发音技巧。建议大家静下心来，跟着熊叔录制的视频、音频，把每个音标都练上两百遍，彻底掌握。

熊叔还在音标练习中搭配了很多国内学习者容易混淆的发音帮大家做区分训练。在学习音标的时候，熊叔也要求大家学会分解每个单词的发音。比如，有鼻音的单词发音都比较难，那你完全可以先去掉鼻音练习这一阶段，然后再把鼻音补回来。例如：sing、song 这两个词的音很难发，那我们先读 si、so 的音，去掉 ng 的音，等练熟后再加上 ng 的音，sing 和 song 的读音就可以发准了。

在音标的发音学习之后，熊叔会带着大家对美式发音的进阶发音技巧进行逐步的训练。这就需要大家在学好发音的基础上再去学进阶的内容。进阶的内容大部分针对词与词之间的连接、句子的节奏把握等。进阶学习之后会进入更高级的篇章朗读训练。熊叔选取了不同题材的内容，包括诗歌、新闻、演讲、歌曲、rap等帮你进行综合训练。整本书建议大家花上 3 个月的时间去学习，学成之后，你的发音一定能够得到很大的改善！

在练习的过程中，熊叔建议大家用以下方法（扫描左侧二维码回复文字"发音练习方法"获取）。

❶ 一定要做到：把自己的声音录下来和熊叔的发音做对比，直到自己满意为止。熊叔在录制的音频／视频中都会有慢速的版本，请大家从慢速版本开始对比，然后再去对比常规语速版本。

❷ 夸张表演法。把一句话，分别用最惊讶、最开心、最痛心、最生气等极端的情绪表演出来。比如，You should have told me.

❸ 嘴巴瑜伽法。把要练习的内容用最慢的语速缓缓地读出来，感受自己口腔肌肉的拉伸。比如，You—should—have—told—me.

❹ 歌唱法。把要练习的内容用自己喜欢的歌的调子唱出来，或者干脆"freestyle"一点，用任何调子唱出来都可以，甚至用说唱来演绎也可以。比如，You should have told me, uh, uh.

❺ 倒车法。把句子从最后一个单词开始读，挨个把前面的单词加回来。这样能够培养重音和弱读的感觉。比如：

me.

told me.

have told me.

should have told me.

You should have told me.

❻ 绕口令法。找含有相应的音标或发音技巧的绕口令进行训练。比如，练习"辅音失去爆破"就可以选择绕口令：How much wood would a woodchuck chuck if a woodchuck could chuck wood.

❼ 标记法。当我们进行连读、弱读等进阶训练的时候，如果你不够熟练，则可以通过标记法，把句子该怎么读标记出来。每个人的标记都可以不一样。比如：

You should have told me. 熊叔喜欢的标记就是 You **should**'ve **told** me. 加粗表示重读，划掉表示失去爆破等。这个方法我们在后期训练连读的时候会专门讲到的。

训练之前的小热身，让你的发音更带感

准备好开始练习发音了吗？我建议大家每次练习发音之前，都花几分钟时间做个小热身，拉伸一下你的口腔肌肉。

热身运动 1：脖子放松，让头部自然下垂，深吸一口气，不间断地发声。你可以发 hmmmmm，可以发 emmm 等，保证声音不间断的同时，用双手去托住自己的下巴，头部、脖子仍然保持放松，用手部的力量抬起我们的头部，让脖子恢复正常的状态。如果你的声音没有间断，你会发现两个姿势下的发声感受完全不一样。

低头的时候我们的气息处于被压迫的状态，恢复正常姿势后气息也跟着恢复正常。用手部力量抬起头是为了让你体验头部的重量。正确的发声方式能够让我们在练习的时候更顺畅地运用我们的发声器官。

热身运动 2：慢慢张大嘴巴，到极限为止，保持住，然后打个大大的哈欠，认真体会打哈欠时喉咙发声的状态。可以多重复几次。这个练习可以帮助我们感受口腔的肌肉变化以及喉咙发声时的状态，让我们在说英语的时候更有底气。

热身运动 3：把一只手放在胸前，另一只手放在鼻子上，然后发出哼鸣声。从你能做到的最低音开始，一路发到你能 hold 住的最高音。如果气息足够，可以继续发到自己能发出的最低音。

发音期间不要间断，仔细体会发音过程中胸腔和鼻腔的共鸣，并尝试记住这种感觉。平时多做这个练习，可能会让你的发音更带感！

关注微信公众号"熊叔英语"，回复"发音热身"，看光头熊叔真人演示。

下面，就让我们开启我们的发音之旅吧！

目　录

1

英语发音的
基础——音标

从本章开始我们正式学习英语发音最基础的部分——音标。

因为国际音标更为大家所熟知，所以熊叔会先介绍大家熟悉的国际音标，然后再附上相对应的美式音标。如果大家是零基础，或者之前没学过音标，就优先学美式音标吧！本书后面的发音技巧中会以美式音标为主。

关注微信公众号"**熊叔英语**"，回复"**音标讲解**"，查看本章内容的视频讲解、收听音频讲解以及跟读训练。

假设你正在跟熊叔显摆你之前去过某个海滩，你本该对熊叔说：Uncle Bear, I went to the **beach** last weekend. 结果呢，因为发音不标准，惹得熊叔哈哈大笑。你对熊叔说的是：Uncle Bear, I went to the **bitch** last weekend.

然后你又跟熊叔说，唉，酒店的床单太脏了，只能要求换个全新的。你本该对服务员说：Hi, can I have a new piece of **sheet**, please? 结果熊叔又哈哈大笑。因为你说的是：Hi, can I have a new piece of **shit**, please?

所以，如果 /iː/ 和 /ɪ/ 这两个音发不准，就会闹出很多笑话。那么，这两个音到底怎么发呢？很多同学会觉得，就是一个长音、一个短音而已。熊叔告诉你，这是大错特错的（我们可以看一下美式音标 /i/ 和 /ɪ/，根本没有代表长音符号的"："）。实际上是这样的：你语速快，长音也会变短音；你语速慢，短音也会变长音。所以这两个音最大的区别，不是发音的长短，而是口型的不同。

元 音

◎ 前元音: /i/, /ɪ/, /ɛ/, /æ/

我们先来学习前元音，英语音标共有四个前元音，国际音标是 /iː/、/ɪ/、/e/、/æ/。对应的美式音标为 /i/、/ɪ/、/ɛ/、/æ/。发音时，舌位的最高点都在舌前部，所以被称为前元音。

🐻 国际音标 /iː/（美式音标 /i/）

◀) 熊叔趣谈发音口型

这个音标的发音与字母"E"发音相同。发音时嘴唇微微咧开一条缝，舌尖抵下齿，舌头前端铆足了劲儿向上抬，嘴角咧向耳朵，露出微笑，这就是为什么外国人在拍照的时候喜欢说 cheese。

需要注意一点，在美式发音当中是没有长、短元音之分的，美式音标中也没有"："这个长音符号。音标的长短更多的是因为语速、重音等叠加因素造成的。

常见字母或字母组合

ee — see, tree

ea — eat, seat

ie —piece, field

e — secret, she

i — police, ski

大声跟着熊叔读

s**ea**t

sh**ee**p

r**ee**se

m**e**

sl**ee**p

f**ee**l

dr**ea**m

英语说唱有嘻哈

Take a seat and listen to me

She loves Reese, and no one

loves me

I'm counting sheep, I can only

sleep

I can feel her again, but she's

only in my dream

熊叔舌头好灵活

See the breeze. 看那微风。

Teasing the tree. 逗趣着树。

Weaving the leaves.

摇晃树叶。

And shaking them free.

自由飘落。

国际音标 /i/（美式音标 /i/）

🔊 熊叔趣谈发音口型

　　还记得军训报数吗？"1,2,3……"中的"1"发音短促而轻快，就好像这个音标的发音。嘴唇微张，舌尖抵下齿，舌头前端仍较高。你会感觉它和 /i/ 的发音差不多，实际上两者并不相同，最明显的区别就是发 /ɪ/ 时嘴巴的内部空间要比发 /i/ 时大一些。

　　这里再次强调，这两个音的区别不是长短之分，而是口型不同！你可以先发 seat，在这个音的基础上，把舌头向下压，让口腔的内部空间更大一些，继而发出 sit。

常见字母或字母组合

i — sit, bit

y — system

e — pretty, blanket

u — busy, business

ui — build, guitar

a — village, private

大声跟着熊叔读

pig

wig

pit

dig

英语说唱有嘻哈

Yo！ Yo！

I'm riding a pig

And I'm wearing a wig

There's a really big pit

I gotta jump over it

熊叔舌头好灵活

I wish to wish the wish you wish to wish, but if you wish the wish the witch wishes, I won't wish the wish you wish to wish.

我愿许下你所许下的愿望，若你的愿望太过虚幻且不切实际，我将不会许你所许的愿望。

对比练习

听一听，熊叔读的是括号里的哪个单词？

- He isn't going to (leave / live).

- Try not to (sleep / slip).

- They want to buy a (sheep / ship).

- Those (heels / hills) are very high.

跟着熊叔大声朗读句子

- He isn't going to leave.

- Try not to slip.

- They want to buy a ship.

- Those heels are very high.

熊叔带你做练习

当我们拍照的时候，不说"yeah"，而说"Cheese"；

当我们不高兴的时候，不说"哎呀我去"，而说"Shit"；

如果你使用的是苹果手机，那么你至少要会说"Hey, Siri❶"；

如果你使用的是三星手机，那么跟我一起念"Hi, Bixby❷"。

---

❶ Siri：iPhone 手机的语音助手。

❷ Bixby：三星手机的语音助手。

经典美句

Everything will be OK in the end, if it's not OK, it's not the end.

所有的事情到最后都会好起来，如果不够好，说明还没有到最后。

国际音标 /e/（美式音标 /ɛ/）

◀)) 熊叔趣谈发音口型

　　跟着熊叔说"谢谢"，说完之后不要动，表情定格后的口型大小就很接近发 /e/ 音时的口型了。发音时嘴巴略微张开，比发短音 /ɪ/ 时嘴巴更大一些，呈扁平形，舌尖抵下齿龈。注意这个音是个短元音，一定要发得干脆利落，发音过程中口型不要有变化。

常见字母或字母组合

e — egg, pen

ea — bread, ready

a — many, any

ie — friend

英语说唱有嘻哈

Forget about the mess

Let's have a rest

East or west

Home is the best

大声跟着熊叔读

mess

rest

west

best

熊叔舌头好灵活

The wet pet in the net hasn't got on the jet plane yet.

网里的湿了的宠物还没有登上喷气飞机。

国际音标 /æ/（美式音标 /æ/）

熊叔趣谈发音口型

　　人在呕吐的时候会尽量把嘴巴张大，拉向两边，舌尖抵下齿龈。汉语中并没有与这个奇葩音标近似的发音，大家可以想象一个婴儿一边流哈喇子一边憨笑时的样子，大概就是那个口型了。

　　目前学到的几个音标当中，发 /æ/ 音时是口腔内部空间最大的。四个音口腔内部空间按从小到大依次排列是：/ɪ/, /i/, /ɛ/, /æ/。

常见字母或字母组合

a — cat, fat, bag

大声跟着熊叔读

f<u>a</u>st

p<u>a</u>ck

c<u>a</u>t

b<u>a</u>g

英语说唱有嘻哈

Be fast! Be fast!

Or this place will be packed!

I'll tell you a secret, Uncle Bear is so fat!

Don't let the cat out of the bag!

熊叔舌头好灵活

Can you can a can as a canner can can a can?

你能像装罐工人一样装罐头吗？

Yes We Can !

对比练习

听一听，熊叔读的是哪个单词？

- bed/bad
- man/men
- pen/pan
- hat/head

跟着熊叔大声朗读句子

- You're so bad.
- I'm your man.
- Do you have a pen?
- He's falling head over heels for her.

熊叔带你做练习

当我们逛街的时候，看到琳琅满目的奢侈品牌，

除了会念香奈儿，还要会念"Chanel"；

除了会读芬迪，还要会读"Fendi"；

别光想着特斯拉，还要会读"Tesla"；

特斯拉太贵就奔驰，奔驰读作"Benz"；

凯迪拉克也不错，凯迪拉克是"Cadillac"。

经典美句

Never frown, even when you are sad, because you never know who is falling in love with your smile.

纵然伤心，也不要愁眉不展，因为你不知道谁会爱上你的笑容。

熊叔教你唱情歌

She said some days I feel like crap

Some days I wanna quit and just be normal for a bit

I don't understand why you have to always be gone

I get along but your trips always feel so long

—*Where'd You Go*

我敢打赌，能用美式发音将"famous""purpose""nervous"等单词读标准的人非常少。很多人觉得美式发音就是用卷舌而已，结果练出的口音虽然流利，实际上却不伦不类。这是为什么呢？

那么，让我们来看一下到底什么是"卷舌音"。

"卷舌音"其实只是类比我们汉语里北方人说话时带有儿化音所说的名词，但实际上英语里的"卷舌音"和汉语里的儿化音差距还是挺大的。美式发音中的"卷舌"，只是舌尖向上翘，而没有真的"卷"到嘴里，相比较而言儿化音更夸张。所以要注意，本书中提到的美式发音中的"卷舌音"只需要让舌尖向鼻子的方向上翘即可。

◎ 中元音：/ɜ˞/，/ɚ/，/ə/

下面我们来学习中元音，在国际音标中，中元音有 /ɜ:/ 和 /ə/，在美式音标中，中元音有 /ɜ˞/、/ɚ/、/ə/（其中后两个音标对应的都是国际音标中 /ə/ 的发音）。发音时，舌位最高点都在中部，舌尖要轻触下齿，嘴巴自然张开。

国际音标 /ɜ:/（美式音标 /ɜ˞/）

◀» 熊叔趣谈发音口型

/ɜ:/ 就是美式音标的 /ɜ˞/，在发这个音的时候，得把您那（nei）

小嘴儿张开，在美音（儿）里，这音（儿）后头经常会加 r 音（儿），就像北京方言里的儿化音，您那（nei）舌头的动作还得带上一个卷儿，但如果是英式发音，就不需要卷舌了。这个音加不加卷舌，是英、美两种发音方式的标志性区别之一（大家可以看出我这段话的腔调是在模仿北京话）。

常见字母或字母组合

or — world, worm

ir — bird, third

er — serve, her

ur — hurt, fur

ear — learn, early

our — journal, courteous

大声跟着熊叔读

ne**r**vous　　注意 vous 这里不卷舌！

nu**r**se

sea**r**ch

chu**r**ch

wo**r**st

earth

英语说唱有嘻哈

A nervous nurse, searching in a church

With the worst work on the earth

She didn't want to make it worse

Her only hope was to find the worm

Which legend foretold could cure her

熊叔舌头好灵活

Sir, your bird stirred my friend's birthday party.

先生，您的鸟搅乱了我朋友的生日派对。

国际音标 /ə/（美式音标 /ɚ/&/ə/）

🔊 熊叔趣谈发音口型

国际音标的 /ə/ 是个短音，如果老师点名让你回答问题，而你又不会，那么你的第一反应也许是"呃……"。发此音时，舌身放平，舌中部隆起，双唇扁平。在这里请大家考虑一个问题：为什么这个国际音标会对应两个美式音标？

因为在美式音标中，这个发音分为卷舌和不卷舌两种情况。简言之，发音的字母组合里有 r 的就卷舌，对应的美式音标是 /ɚ/。发音的字母或字母组合里没有 r 的，就不卷舌，对应的美式音标是 /ə/。

/ɚ/：发音字母组合中有字母 r，卷舌，如 mother、father 中的 er。

/ə/：发音字母或字母组合中没有字母 r，不卷舌，如 famous、nervous 中的 ou。

常见字母或字母组合	大声跟着熊叔读
a — **a**bout, m**a**chine	fath**er**
e — sev**e**n, happ**e**n	moth**er**
o — **o**ccasion, c**o**llect	oth**er**
er — gov**er**n, sist**er**	ev**er**
or — f**or**get, doct**or**	

英语说唱有嘻哈

My father and mother

So in love with each other

More than 40 years together

Their love could be forever

熊叔舌头好灵活

The bottom of the butter bucket

is the buttered bucket bottom.

黄油桶桶底是抹上了黄油的

桶底。

对比练习

对比下列读音，哪些需要卷舌，哪些不需要卷舌？

- p**ur**p**o**se, p**er**fect
- ad**a**m, ladd**er**
- tend**er**, pand**a**
- f**ur**th**er**, both**er**, res**ear**ch**er**

跟着熊叔大声朗读句子

- Everyone has a purpose in life.
- Don't be nervous, just give it a shot.
- Look at that panda! I wish I could raise a panda myself.
- No one is perfect. Not Adam, not Uncle Bear.

熊叔带你做练习

职场交流的必会英文，你都说对了吗？

例如，领导会说 Uncle Bear，给我一份你的 plan forward，CC 给你的 leader。

Robert，你是个 sales，有点 sense 好吗，要更 aggressive 一点好吗？

现在就跟着熊叔一起学习：forward，leader，Robert，aggressive。

经典美句

I want to give you all the best in the world, only to find the best in the world is you.

我想把世界上最好的都给你，却发现这世界上最好的就是你。

熊叔教你唱情歌

Come on over in my direction

So thankful for that it's such a blessin' yeah

Turn every situation into heaven yeah

Oh you are

My sunrise on the darkest day

Got me feelin' some kind of way

Make me wanna savor every moment slowly slowly

—*Despacito*

　　假设你和一个外国友人一起吃饭，吃完后外国友人问你有没有吃饱。你说：I'm full. 结果话音刚落外国友人便放声大笑说：You what? 因为你说成了：I'm fool. 而且还是个病句，少了冠词 a。这就好比一个老外说"我吃过了"，结果开口却说成了"我蠢了"。

◎ 后元音：/u/，/ʊ/，/ɑr/，/ʌ/，/ɔr/，/ɔ/，/ɑ/

　　英语音标共有七个后元音，国际音标是 /uː/、/ʊ/、/ɑː/、/ɒ/、/ɔː/、/ɒ/、/ʌ/[1]，对应的美式音标为 /u/、/ʊ/、/ɑr/、/ɑ/、/ɔr/、/ɔ/、/ʌ/。同

---

[1]　有些资料中这个音也会被归类到中元音中，但实际发声位置靠后，且国人非常容易把这个音和 /ɑ/ 弄混，为了方便对比，本书中暂归类到后元音中讲解。

样我们会发现，在美式音标当中，长音符号没有了。发音时，舌位最高点都在后部，舌头向后缩，舌尖离开下齿，嘴巴自然张开。

国际音标 /u:/（美式音标 /u/）

🔊 熊叔趣谈发音口型

升堂！"威——武——"其中"武"发一声调，和 /u:/ 的发音有些相近。拖长音，上下齿微微分开，嘴型小而圆，微微外凸，舌头尽量后缩。或者我们也可以想象人在想要接吻时的口型，微微噘起嘴唇，等待浪漫的那一刻。

常见字母或字母组合

u — rule, June

o — tomb, prove

oo — pool, school

ou — soup, group

ui — juice, fruit

ew — drew, grew

大声跟着熊叔读

food

school

noon

fool

英语说唱有嘻哈

You bring some food to school

You eat the food at noon

But are you not a fool

You eat noodle with a spoon

熊叔舌头好灵活

The wolf in wool rested on the tool stool in the zoo.

穿羊毛大衣的狼在动物园里的工具凳子上歇息。

国际音标 /ʊ/（美式音标 /ʊ/）

🔊 熊叔趣谈发音口型

　　此音为短音，发音时嘴唇张开，略向前突出，嘴型稍圆，肌肉放松一些，舌头往后缩，舌尖离开下齿。

　　发 /ʊ/ 音时口腔内部空间大于发 /u:/（美式音标 /u/）音时的空间。

　　同样的，在美式发音中，前面学过的这两个音标也没有长短之分，而是在口型上有区别。发 /ʊ/ 时的口腔内部空间是要大于

发 /u/ 的。你可以在发 /u/ 的基础上，舌头下压，让口腔内部空间变大，发出 /ʊ/ 音。

常见字母或字母组合

u — sugar, push

o — wolf, woman

oo — foot, look

ou — could, would

英语说唱有嘻哈

Look at that woman

Pushing the door open

By hook and crook

She's a gorgeous woman

大声跟着熊叔读

look

woman

push

book

熊叔舌头好灵活

How many cookies could a good cook cook if a good cook could cook cookies?

如果一个好厨师能做饼干，那么他能做多少个饼干呢？

对比练习

听一听，区分出哪些是长音，哪些是短音？

- cookie, cook, cool
- good, hook, true
- loot, drool, tool
- root, rude, wool

跟着熊叔大声朗读句子

- The cook is cool.
- Her words are good and true.
- Don't be rude!
- How could the cook cook so many cookies in two minutes?

熊叔带你做练习

　　曾经，有一位可爱的阿姨跟熊叔聊过她去加拿大购物的经历，她说："I buy a goose."

　　我问："你买了只鹅回来吗？鹅吗？活的？"阿姨开始用上海话问她老公："阿拉易老 Canada 马了撒么斯？"阿姨的老公在边上说："你要说那是衣服牌子的呀！裙子呀！"阿姨恍然大悟，改口道："I buy a goose dress."

　　云里雾里了一阵之后，我灵光一闪，问阿姨："Goose 是指 Gucci？"阿姨说："对呀，就是 Gucci（goose）呀！不是什么大鹅呀，哈哈。"（以上对话，阿姨不仅发错了 Gucci 的音，还用错了时态！）

　　请大声朗读：Gucci，Louis Vuitton。

经典美句

If I could take one thing away from us, it would be distance.

如果我能拿走一样我们的东西，那肯定是距离。

熊叔教你唱情歌

But I got smarter I got harder in the nick of time

Honey I rose up from the dead I do it all the time

I got a list of names and yours is in red underlined

I check it once then I check it twice ooh

Ooh look what you made me do

Look what you made me do

Look what you just made me do

Look what you just made me

Ooh look what you made me do

Look what you made me do

Look what you just made me do

Look what you just made me do

I don't like your kingdom keys

—Look What You Mode Me Do

国际音标 /ɑ:/（美式音标 /ɑr/）

熊叔趣谈发音口型

　　假如你的嗓子发炎了，去看医生时，医生让你张开嘴巴，发出"啊——"，与此同时，医生要看你的扁桃体，把医疗用具伸进你的嘴里，于是你的嘴巴还要尽量张大，舌头吓得往后缩，口腔肌肉紧绷，发出长长的"啊"音。当音节中有"r"字母时，记得要带上儿化音。注意，类似于 last、glass、dance 等这类词，在英式发音当中会发 /ɑ:/，但在美音当中会发 /æ/。

常见字母或字母组合

a — last, glass（美式发音 /læst/, /glæs/）

ar — far, smart

al — calf, behalf（美式发音 /kæf/,/bɪˈhæf/）

au — aunt（美式发音 /ænt/）

ear — heart

大声跟着熊叔读

f**a**st（美式发音 /fæst/)

c**ar**

p**ar**k

h**ear**t

英语说唱有嘻哈

It was the first time for me to drive a car

I didn't know how to hit the brake or park the car

I lost my glasses and I couldn't feel my heart

I lost all my hair, and I needed to go to a bar

熊叔舌头好灵活

Can you drive the large car to the far bar?

你能把这台大型的车开到远方的酒吧吗？

国际音标 /ʌ/（美式音标 /ʌ/）

有一次，我的一个好友跟一个外国朋友一起吃火锅，点餐的时候，外国朋友说想要"blood"。好友说："服务员，要一份鸭血。"外国朋友说："我说的是锅底要不辣的。"

为何会出现这种状况呢？因为好友把 blood 的 /ʌ/ 音听错了！

🔊 熊叔趣谈发音口型

此音为短音，请放松脸部肌肉，嘴唇微张，舌尖轻触下齿，舌后部稍稍抬起。/ʌ/ 的发音跟"啊"的发音其实没有什么关系，它的发音有点类似前面学过的 /ə/。常见的错误是，很多同学在发这个音的时候嘴巴张得很大，其实它的口型很小，嘴巴张开的程度和发 /ə/ 音时差不多。

常见字母或字母组合

u — cut, ugly, uncle

o — become, monkey

oo — flood, blood

ou — rough, country

大声跟着熊叔读

d<u>u</u>ck

bl<u>oo</u>d

en<u>ou</u>gh

y<u>u</u>m

英语说唱有嘻哈

It was the first time my friend saw blood

But then she said she liked it and it was not enough

I was so shocked that she turned out to be a vampire

So I cooked the duck blood till it became yum yum

熊叔舌头好灵活

The customers are accustomed to the disgusting custom.

顾客们习惯了这令人讨厌的风俗。

对比练习

听一听，熊叔读的是哪个单词？

- cut/cart
- duck/dark
- flood/fled
- rough/Ralf

跟着熊叔大声朗读句子

- I can't see the duck because it's too dark!
- They fled before the flood.
- Rough winds do shake the darling buds of May. (Sonnets 18，出自十四行诗的第 18 首）
- Put the scissors in the shopping cart. I need to cut something.

熊叔带你做练习

在英语中，凡是句子中有 but 的，but 后面的内容往往更重要。比如，熊叔去表白，对方说：

Uncle Bear, you are a terrific guy, but... (I don't wanna spend my life with someone bald.)

熊叔去跟老板申请涨工资，老板说：

Uncle Bear, you've done a great job, but... (I don't wanna give a raise to someone bald.)

熊叔去跟朋友借钱，朋友说：

Uncle Bear, I would lend you $500, but... (I don't wanna lend money to someone bald.)

经典美句

The problem of your past is your business, the problem of your future is my privilege.

你的过去我来不及参与，你的未来我奉陪到底。

熊叔教你唱情歌

cuz it's too much (cuz 为 because 的缩写形式)

Yeah it's a lot

to be something I'm not

I'm a fool

out of love

cuz I just can't get enough

—*The Show*

国际音标 /ɔ:/（美式音标 /ɔr/）

◄) 熊叔趣谈发音口型

　　人在恍然大悟的时候，往往会发出一声悠长的"噢——"，这个发音便有点接近 /ɔ:/ 的发音（注意只是接近）。发此音时，双唇收得小而圆，舌身往后缩，肌肉也跟着紧张起来。在美式发音中，如果字母组合中有字母 r，需要加上卷舌音来收尾。如果字母组合中没有字母 r，那么只需要发 /ɔ/，仍然没有长音符号。

常见字母或字母组合

a— almost, also（本组合在美音中发 /ɔ/，不卷舌）

or — north, short

au — audio, autumn（本组合在美音中发 /ɔ/，不卷舌）

ar — war, quarter

aw — paw, law（本组合在美音中发 /ɔ/，不卷舌）

oor — floor, door

---

our — four, source

oar — aboard, boar

augh — caught, daughter（本组合在美音中发 /ɔ/，不卷舌）

ough — bought, fought（本组合在美音中发 /ɔ/，不卷舌）

大声跟着熊叔读

p**or**k

c**or**n

c**or**ner

sw**or**d

英语说唱有嘻哈

Tonight for dinner we serve beef and pork

Together with some tuna salad and sweet corn

We don't have chopsticks, so if you need a fork

You can go find it over there in the corner

熊叔舌头好灵活

Knife and a fork, bottle and a cork that is the way you spell New York.

小刀和叉、瓶和软木塞，这就是你拼写纽约的方式。

国际音标 /ɒ/（美式音标 /ɔ/ 或者 /ɑ/）

熊叔趣谈发音口型

　　此音为短音，发音时嘴巴张开的程度要比长音 /ɔ:/ 略大，肌肉自然放松，发音短促而有力。在美音里，一般此音被发成 /ɑ/，例如，hot；在少数情况下发 /ɔ/，例如，dog。

常见字母或字母组合

o — hot, box, God

a — quality, father

大声跟着熊叔读

boss 美音发 /bɔs/

cock

jolly

fox

英语说唱有嘻哈

Uncle Bear is a boss

He has lots of cocks

And a jolly fox

What does the fox say

熊叔舌头好灵活

You cross a cross across a cross, or stick a cross across a cross.

你把一个十字架穿在十字架上，或者把一个十字架贴在十字架上。

对比练习

听一听，熊叔读的是哪个单词？

· cops/corpse

· fox/forks

· house/horse

· war/what

跟着熊叔大声朗读句子

- There are so many cops on the street.
- There're no foxes here.
- The house is on fire.
- The war is finally over.

熊叔带你做练习

找个外国朋友，请他 / 她吃饭！那么，关于餐饮的一些常用语该怎么说呢？

火锅：hot pot

麻辣烫（可以理解为麻辣的火锅）：spicy hot pot

烧烤、烤串：barbecue

路边的特色小吃：local specialty

馄饨：wonton

经典美句

Sometimes, silence hurts more than words.

有时候，沉默比语言更伤人。

熊叔教你唱情歌

How easy it would be to show me how you feel

More than words is all you have to do to make it real

Then you wouldn't have to say that you love me

Cuz I'd already know

What would you do if my heart was torn in two

More than words to show you feel

That your love for me is real

—*More Than Words*

◎ 双元音（合口）：/aɪ/，/e/，/aʊ/，/o/，/ɔɪ/

综述

双元音，顾名思义，是由两个单元音组成的。那么就会涉及从第一个口型到第二个口型的滑动。要注意，在汉语中我们是没有这种可以滑来滑去的音的，所以在练习双元音时，一定要记得口型的滑动要自然、圆润。通俗地讲，就是双元音的发音要有口型滑动的过程。

情景一

假设街头一个帅气的外国人问你："Do you know how to go to Mount Tai(泰山)？"

你一脸茫然地说："毛……茅台？Good good drink...好好喝！"

外国人也一脸茫然道："What? No way!"

你还是一脸茫然地说："This is Chai Na! Not 挪威！"

情景二

曾经有一位学生告诉熊叔，有首英文歌曲是歌唱"内蒙之爱"的。

熊叔瞬间茫然，问同学："我怎么不知道？歌词是怎么唱的呢？"

这位同学清了清嗓子，引吭高歌道："In the 内蒙 love—In the 内蒙 love..."

熊叔忍不住对他翻白眼，那首歌曲的名字明明是 *In the Name of Love*。

国际音标 /aɪ/ （美式音标 /aɪ/）

🔊 熊叔趣谈发音口型

　　"你们爱熊叔吗？""爱！"注意！很多人会觉得 /aɪ/ 的发音就等同于汉字"爱"的发音，这是非常错误的！发 /aɪ/ 音时，先把 /a/ 的音发得饱满、圆润，再滑向 /ɪ/ 的音，要注意口型从开到合的全过程，表情要尽量做到位。在练习的时候，尽量放慢，可以尝试用 5 秒的时间去完成这个发音，去感受自己拉伸口腔肌肉的感觉，给自己的嘴巴做一个瑜伽，体会嘴巴在空中画圈的感觉。

常见字母或字母组合

i — nice, bike

y — style, type

igh — light, sight

大声跟着熊叔读

qu**i**et

n**igh**t

w**i**fe

f**i**ve

英语说唱有嘻哈

It was a very quiet night, in the bed was my wife

We got married in 2005, I'll love her till the end of time
The kids were downstairs, they just turned off the light
Now the night was ours, we were gonna talk about what the future would be like

熊叔舌头好灵活

I like to ride my light white bike, and fly a white light kite with my wife.

我喜欢和妻子骑白色的轻便自行车，放白色的风筝。

国际音标 /eɪ/（美式音标 /e/）

◀) 熊叔趣谈发音口型

假设在办公室里，上司喊了你的名字，你会吓一大跳，并且在第一时间回答："诶——老板您说。"这时你发出了类似（只是类似）字母"A"的声音，但是发声过程有区别。口型由半开到合，从 /e/ 滑到 /ɪ/，发音从强到弱，从长到短，自然过渡。同样的，在练习时把速度放慢，尽可能把口型做到位。

常见字母或字母组合

a — place, same

ey — hey, grey

ay — day, Monday

eigh — weight, eight

大声跟着熊叔读

h**ey**

sh**a**pe

d**ay**

英语说唱有嘻哈

Hey, hey, hey

Hey, hey, hey

I'm in love with the shape of you, eh

I hope I can meet you every day, eh

You dress up like you're only 28, eh

Girl, what ya doin' this Saturday, eh

Come with me I'll show you the best DJ, eh

We'll dance, and we'll never leave till Monday, eh

熊叔舌头好灵活

The rain in Spain is mainly on the plain.

西班牙主要是在平原地区下雨。

对比练习

听一听，熊叔读的是哪个单词？

- shape/sharp
- late/light
- bat/bite
- bit/bait

跟着熊叔大声朗读句子

- Uncle Bear is out of shape.
- The light's off! You're late again!
- The Batman got bitten by a bat.
- We can use the food as bait.

熊叔带你做练习

　　1. 情景一　工作中的你

　　Deadline 又要到了。其实 deadline 并没有带给你爆发式的完成工作的动力，只是给了你把完成的工作用 E-mail 发送出去的勇气。

2. 情景二　大学里的你

老师布置的任务是下个礼拜五分小组做一个关于"×××"的 presentation。到了周四，你忽然发现天哪，明天有个 presentation 我还没有准备啊！ It's too late! 当然，结果是你的英语老师给了你一个 fail。

3. 当面对外国人的时候，你可以自豪地介绍自己：

I'm from China!

I'm Chinese!

I'm from Beijing!

I'm from Shanghai!

经典美句

Someday, you will find the one, who will listen to the rhythm of falling rain with you throughout your life.

总有一天你会遇上那个人，陪着你倾听你人生中的每一次落雨。

熊叔教你唱情歌

Listen to the rhythm of the falling rain

Telling me just what a fool I've been

I wish that it would go and let me cry in vain

And let me be alone again

The only girl I've ever loved has gone away

Looking for a brand new start

But little does she know that when she left that day

Along with her she took my heart

—*Rhythm of the Rain*

国际音标 /aʊ/（美式音标 /aʊ/）

🔊 熊叔趣谈发音口型

设想自己已经七天没吃饭了，饥饿的你发出了这样的号叫："啊呜——"此时的你有多饥饿，发出 /a/ 音时的嘴巴就张开得有多大；此时的你有多虚弱，口型向 /ʊ/ 过渡时就收得有多小。或者你也可以想象自己是一头猛虎，在大声嘶吼。体会口型逐渐由大到小的变化。还记得著名歌手蕾哈娜演唱的歌曲"潍坊的爱"吗？其实歌名是 *We Found Love*。这个双元音在发音时需要尽可能地将嘴巴张开，体会嘴巴在空中慢慢画圈的感觉。

常见字母或字母组合

ou — ground, sound

ow — towel, powder

大声跟着熊叔读

v**ow**

cr**ow**d

n**ow**

h**ou**se

英语说唱有嘻哈

At the altar we exchanged vows

We heard endless applause from the crowd

You and I, we're one family now

I'll work hard, and we'll move in a large house

熊叔舌头好灵活

The sow, the mouse and the cow sang a rousing song.

母猪、老鼠和奶牛唱了一首欢快的歌。

国际音标 /əʊ/（美式音标 /o/）

🔊 熊叔趣谈发音口型

"OK"和"欧了"中的"o"和"欧"的发音，看似接近，其实差别很大。发 /əʊ/ 音时口型自然从扁平到变圆，同样的，第一个音 /ə/ 长而强，第二个音 /ʊ/ 短而弱。体会一下拉长这个双元音的感受，尝试用 5 秒的时间去练习这个发音吧。

常见字母或字母组合

o — open, most

oa — coat, road

ou — soul, shoulder

ow — low, slow

大声跟着熊叔读

cold

hope

home

polar

英语说唱有嘻哈

It's so cold

I have no hope

Just wanna go home

I am not a polar bear

熊叔舌头好灵活

The bold folk fold up the gold and hold it in hand.

大胆的人们将黄金折叠起来拿在手里。

对比练习

听一听，熊叔读的是哪个单词？

- no/now
- so/saw
- go/gal
- howard/hold

跟着熊叔大声朗读句子

- No, the time is not now.
- So, Uncle Bear saw his girlfriend with another man.
- Gals, let's go!
- Yes, Howard, please hold on.

熊叔带你做练习

　　1. 大家现在应该能地道、标准地发出"Oh my God!"了吧。

　　2. 领导在开动员大会的时候喜欢说的一句话：就是现在了！The time is now！或者，Now is the time！大家可以感受一下，这句话的英语版本让两个双元音夸张地表现出来会更加有气势！

3. 很多 80 后、90 后的回忆：*Frozen Throne*（《冰封王座》）。大家可以大声朗读 frozen 和 throne 这两个单词，来感受双元音 /əu/。

4. 推荐几部好看的欧美剧：

How I Met Your Mother《老爸老妈浪漫史》

Two Broke Girls《破产姐妹》

House of Cards《纸牌屋》

IT Crowd《IT 狂人》

经典美句

Don't let someone who doesn't know your value tell you how much you're worth.

别让那些不懂得珍惜你的人来衡量你的价值。

国际音标 /ɔɪ/（美式音标 /ɔɪ/）

🔊 熊叔趣谈发音口型

如果你到了澳大利亚，应该能够经常听到这个音，/ɔ/ 和 /ɪ/ 连在一起发音，口型从圆变扁，前音长而强，后音短而弱。想象嘴巴从吃棒棒糖的口型逐渐变成皮笑肉不笑的表情。

常见字母或字母组合

oy — toy, enjoy

oi — avoid, voice

大声跟着熊叔读

b**oy**

destr**oy**

n**oi**se

av**oi**d

英语说唱有嘻哈

Look at all these toys

You're spoiling your boys

I know their childhood you don't want to destroy

They're making a lot of noise

This life you don't really enjoy

There's something you just can't avoid

熊叔舌头好灵活

The spoiled boy lost his toy and made a lot of noise.

这个被宠坏了的男孩，弄丢了他的玩具，于是就开始嗷嗷乱叫。

熊叔教你唱情歌

The snow glows white on the mountain tonight

Not a footprint to be seen

A kingdom of isolation

And it looks like I'm the Queen

The wind is howling like this swirling storm inside

Couldn't keep it in, heaven knows I've tried

— Let It Go

◎ 双元音（集中双元音）：/ɪə/，/ɪə/，/ɪr/，/ɛr/，/ʊr/

idea、area 这两个单词用美式发音要怎么读呢？这两个词的结尾要不要卷舌？之前熊叔在上课的时候，有的同学经常会叫错我的名字。有些同学会把 Uncle Bear 叫成 Uncle Beer。于是便闹了笑话，熊叔变成了啤酒叔。

这一部分的音标大家需要注意：美式发音分卷舌、不卷舌两种音，其对应的国际音标是一样的。

国际音标 /ɪə/（美式音标 /ɪə/ 或 /iə/ 或 /ɪr/）

🔊 熊叔趣谈发音口型

　　我们先来了解一下为什么音标 /ɪə/ 会有对应的三种美式音标：首先，国际音标中的 /ɪə/ 对应的美式发音有两种，卷舌音和不卷舌音。大部分属于卷舌音，如 /ɪr/，少部分为不卷舌的发音。在美式音标中，从严格意义上来讲，音标 /iə/ 和 /ɪə/ 并不是双元音，而是元音 /i/、/ɪ/ 和 /ə/ 音分别组合在一起而形成的类似于双元音的发音。含有该音标的词汇并不多，如刚刚提到的 idea、area 等。在发音时，我们只需要发对 /ɪr/ 的音，在不需要发卷舌音的时候，只要把尾音落在 /ə/ 上就可以了。

　　在发这个双元音的时候，大家首先要把自己当成一个北京人，口型的起点是我们最开始学的微笑的发音，慢慢向儿化音、卷舌音过渡。当然，英语中的卷舌音也并不是要求大家真的把舌头卷成寿司那样，我们只需要把舌尖上翘，稍微往里卷一点儿就可以了。不得不说，北方人发这个音有天然的优势，南方的小伙伴们可能得听听相声来找找感觉了。注意在美式发音中，没有字母 r 就不要卷舌！

常见字母或字母组合

ea — idea, area（不卷舌）

eer — peer, beer

ere — mere, here

大声跟着熊叔读

h**ere**

ear

re**a**lly（不卷舌）

ser**iou**s（不卷舌）

英语说唱有嘻哈

You wanna a couple of beers

We can't talk here

The walls have ears

You can't be serious

Where should we go

You've got any ideas

熊叔舌头好灵活

The bearded bear will bear a dear baby in the rear.

这个长胡子的熊将在后方生下一头可爱的小熊崽儿。

国际音标 /eə/（美式音标 /ɛr/）

熊叔趣谈发音口型

一定要注意！发这个双元音口型的起点是 bed 中的 /ɛ/，一定要和上面的 /ɪr/ 区别开来，否则你就同那个把 Uncle Bear 叫成 Uncle Beer 的人犯了一样的错误！嘴巴自然张开，脸部肌肉紧张，发 /ɛ/，向卷舌音过渡，练习时可以拉长这个音。发完此音要记得翘起舌尖。

常见字母或字母组合

are — compare, dare

air — hair, fair

ear — wear, pear

大声跟着熊叔读

c**are**

r**are**

w**ear**

h**air**

b**ear**

英语说唱有嘻哈

Uncle Bear has no hair

But he doesn't really care

He doesn't need to take care of his hair

And all kinds of wigs he can wear

Sometimes Uncle Bear likes to sing

But it just wouldn't be fair

Cuz his singing is terrible

Something even you can't really bear

熊叔舌头好灵活

I met a fairly unfair affair upstairs.

我在楼上遇见了一件很不公平的事。

对比练习

听一听，熊叔读的是哪个单词？

- bear/bell/beer
- fare/fear/fell
- Clair/clear
- hair/here

跟着熊叔大声朗读句子

- Uncle Bear doesn't drink beer.

- Never fear Uncle Bear.

- Clair made it clear that she wasn't going to marry Uncle Bear.

- Clair has nice hair, but Uncle Bear has no hair.

熊叔带你做练习

长发及腰：waist-long hair

齐肩长发：shoulder-length hair

直发：straight hair

鬈发：curly hair

光头：shaved head（刮出来的）

秃头：bald head（脱发脱的）

小清新的马尾辫：pony tail

辫子：braid

大波浪：wave hair

樱桃小丸子头：bob

精灵烫：pixie cut

爆炸头：afro

极具个性的莫西干发型：mohawk

平头：crew cut

中分：center parting

侧分：side parting

刘海：bangs

经典美句

All I can do is try to hold on to both of us somewhere inside of me.

我所能做的就是试着在心灵深处紧紧地守候着你。

center parting
pony tail

bangs
braid

side parting
wave hair

pixie cut

afro

mohawk

国际音标 /ʊə/（美式音标 /ʊr/）

◀》 熊叔趣谈发音口型

提到乌鸡，大家应该并不会感到陌生。那么，我们把乌鸡的"鸡"字换成"鹅"字来读一读，"乌鹅"的发音便与音标 /ʊə/ 的发音比较类似。把 /ʊ/ 和 /ə/ 连在一起发音（美式音标 /ʊr/），口型从收圆到半开，想象口型从亲吻别人的样子逐渐滑动到淡定地自然张开嘴巴的状态。发对应的美式音标的时候，不要忘记在最后加上一个儿化音。

常见字母或字母组合

ure — sure, assure

oor — poor, boor

our — tour

大声跟着熊叔读

broch**ure**

t**our**

c**ure**

sec**ure**

英语说唱有嘻哈

Being poor is a sickness for

which no one has cure

Especially when you wanna

go to Europe for a tour

Checking all the great places

out on the brochure

You realize there's something

you have to make sure

Work harder, learn harder,

then you find the cure

Find a boyfriend who's gonna

make you feel secure

Then every day in your life is

a different kind of tour

熊叔舌头好灵活

The impure mixture with impurity is purified.

含杂质的混合物被提纯了。

对比练习

听一听，熊叔读的是哪个单词？

- poor/pork
- sure/show
- cure/cord
- tours/towards

跟着熊叔大声朗读句子

He's so poor that he can't afford the pork.

Are you sure? I could show you around.

Scientists just found the cure for cancer.

I'm taking a tour in Paris. I'm walking towards the Eiffel Tower.

熊叔教你唱情歌

But that's just how the story unfolds

You get another hand soon after you fold

And when your plans unravel in the sand

What would you wish for, if you had one chance

So airplane airplane sorry I'm late

I'm on my way so don't close that gate

If I don't make that then I'll switch my flight and

I'll be right back at it by the end of the night

Can we pretend that airplanes in the night sky are like shootin' stars

I could really use a wish right now, wish right now, wish right now

Can we pretend that airplanes in the night sky are like shootin' stars

I could really use a wish right now, wish right now, wish right now

—Airplanes

辅音

想听熊叔练了很久的 beatbox 吗？我们大家一起来读一读：boots，cats，boots，cats，boots，cats，boots，cats，boom，boom，cats.

看辅音之前先来学两个概念：清辅音和浊辅音。清辅音就是声带不振动的辅音，浊辅音就是声带振动的辅音。判断的方法很简单，男孩子把手放在喉结处，发音时如果那里振动的那就是浊音，不振动的就是清音。女孩子请把自己当成男孩子，然后假装自己有个喉结就可以了。

◎ **爆破音**：/p/，/b/，/t/，/d/，/k/，/g/

国际音标 /p/（美式音标 /p/）

🔊 **熊叔趣谈发音口型**

此音标的发音不同于汉语拼音"p"的发音，大家千万不要受母语的影响。拼音"P"发"泼"的音，短促而轻快地发声，声带不发出声音。而紧闭嘴唇，然后用气流突然冲出双唇，发出一个爆破音来，就是 /p/ 的发音。这是一个清辅音，声带不需要振动。

常见字母或字母组合

p — pen, public

pp — suppose, appear

大声跟着熊叔读

paint

picture

piece

pa**p**er

pretty

英语说唱有嘻哈

She paints a picture on a piece of paper

As a pretty present to her handsome husband

Her husband doesn't like it, but he says it's perfect

She doesn't want to tell him now, but she bought it from Taobao

熊叔舌头好灵活

Peter Piper picked a peck of pickled peppers. A peck of pickled peppers Peter Piper picked. If Peter Piper picked a peck of pickled peppers, where's the peck of pickled peppers Peter Piper picked?

彼得·派柏捏起一撮泡菜。彼得·派柏捏起的是一撮泡菜。如果彼得·派柏捏起的是一撮泡菜，那么彼得·派柏捏起的泡菜在哪儿？

国际音标 /b/（美式音标 /b/）

🔊 熊叔趣谈发音口型

此音标的发音区别于汉语拼音"bo"或是汉字"波"的发音，发音时要尽量干脆利落。口型（or 唇形）和发 /p/ 音时一模一样，声带振动，就是 /b/ 的发音。

常见字母或字母组合

b — robot, back

bb — stubborn, ribbon

大声跟着熊叔读

bear

a**b**sent

because

backache

英语说唱有嘻哈

Can you bear a bear as a bear can bear a bear

Bears are born smart,

they can feel if you are scared

So the best thing for you to do

is to play dead if you dare

熊叔舌头好灵活

The bear could not bear the boar. The boar thought the bear a bore.

熊不能忍受野猪，野猪又嫌熊烦。

对比练习

听一听，熊叔读的是哪个单词？

- play/clay
- put/boot
- pot/but
- mop/mob

跟着熊叔大声朗读句子

- The artist is playing with clay.
- Where did you put my boots?
- Let's go to a hot pot restaurant!
- I'll make a mop out of your waist-long hair.

熊叔带你做练习

please 在英文中是非常常见的词。为了彰显绅士风度，我们可以在很多地方加上 please 这个词。比如：

Could you bring me some water, please?

Where is the Empire State Building, please?

Have dinner with me, please.

Finish the report by Monday, please.

有一首英文歌，我想大家应该都很熟悉，这首歌有一整段歌词都是由"baby"这一个单词组成的，如下：

Baby, baby, baby, oh

Baby, baby, baby, oh

Baby, baby, baby, oh

经典美句

There is no good and evil, there is only power and those too weak to seek it.

世上并没有绝对的善与恶，差别只在于强者和无法分清事实的弱者。

👤 国际音标 /t/（美式音标 /t/）

🔊 熊叔趣谈发音口型

首先，我们要注意不要把这个音发成中文的"特"。舌尖舔你上面的两个门牙后面，堵住气流，然后让气流突然爆破冲出你的舌尖和门牙之间，发出这个音。可以把手掌放在嘴巴前面，发 /t/ 音的时候会有气流冲到手掌上。在美式英语中，如果 t 是单词首字母，往往这个 /t/ 的音会稍微重一些。另外，在美式发音中，如果 /t/ 是在"非重度闭音节"的开头，会被读成不送气的 /t/。具体情况比较复杂，后面熊叔会用一整个章节给大家详细讲解。

常见字母或字母组合

t — tall, tell

tt — pretty, attack

大声跟着熊叔读

tomorrow

whatever

setback

英语说唱有嘻哈

Love me and trust me

tomorrow will be fine

This is only a setback you

don't really need to cry

Whatever happens I'm gonna

be there in your life

So calm down and carry on,

everything will be all right

熊叔舌头好灵活

Betty bought some butter, but

she said the butter's bitter. If I

put it in my batter, it will make

my batter bitter.

贝蒂买了些黄油，但她说黄油

有点苦。如果我把黄油放进甜

饼糊，它会使甜饼糊变苦。

国际音标 /d/（美式音标 /d/）

熊叔趣谈发音口型

　　首先，我们要注意不要把这个音发成汉字"得"音。和发 /t/ 音

时的口型一样，此外，发 /d/ 音的时候要使声带振动。

常见字母或字母组合

d — down, blind

dd — muddy, sudden

大声跟着熊叔读

<u>d</u>o

<u>d</u>epen<u>d</u>

goo<u>d</u>

<u>d</u>ay

英语说唱有嘻哈

Do what you wanna do, be what you wanna be

A good day starts with being happy

Read books, learn English when you are free

Live a healthy life and have a nice dream in your sleep

熊叔舌头好灵活

The man beyond the bond is fond of the second wonderful diamond.

那位不受约束的人喜欢第二颗奇异的钻石。

对比练习

听一听，熊叔读的是哪个单词？

- tie/die/buy/pie
- down/town
- do/to
- not/nod

59

跟着熊叔大声朗读句子

• He's wearing a beautiful tie.

• Uncle Bear doesn't work in downtown Shanghai.

• What do we do to the people we love?

• In some places, nodding your head means no.

熊叔带你做练习

在北京、上海、广州、深圳这样的城市里，很多人其实是工作在市区（downtown），生活在郊区（suburb）的。每天的上、下班方式是：先走路（walk）、再坐公交车（bus），最后还要乘坐地铁（subway）。有些时候当你等 bus 等得时间很久，终于打车（take a taxi）了之后，发现远处两辆 bus 一起来了。

在国外流行的打车软件叫"Uber"，我们国内最为流行的打车软件是"Didi"。

下面我们来看一下几种常见的"车"的英文表达。

快车：express

出租车：taxi

顺风车：free ride/hitchhike/carpool

代驾：designated driver

自驾租车：car rental

经典美句

One should love animals, because they are our friends.

每个人都应该热爱动物，因为它们是我们的朋友。

国际音标 /k/（美式音标 /k/）

🔊 熊叔趣谈发音口型

这个音标的发音和汉字"科"的发音有相近的地方。发音时，舌头中后部拱起，顶着嘴巴上面（上颚），让拱起来的舌头和嘴巴在深处形成一个小而封闭的空间，然后突然爆发，气流冲出，在你的嘴里吐出一口气，发出这个音。

常见字母或字母组合

k — key, kick

c — can, cry

ck — duck, dick

cc — accuse, account

大声跟着熊叔读

come

like

cry

英语说唱有嘻哈

Come on, come on, turn the radio on

It's Uncle Bear, and it won't be long

Is he singing a song

I must have heard it wrong

He sings like he's crying

He sounds like a gong

熊叔舌头好灵活

Blake's black bike's back brake bracket block broke.

布雷克的黑色自行车的后闸托架快坏了。

国际音标 /g/（美式音标 /g/）

熊叔趣谈发音口型

我们想象一下武松在打虎之前，老虎凶猛地对着武松低吼："geeeeee"。/g/ 的发音口型和 /k/ 一样，但是声带振动。

常见字母或字母组合

g — go, bug

gg — struggle, beggar

gu — guard, guest

大声跟着熊叔读

go

a**g**ain

get

na**g**

英语说唱有嘻哈

Here I go again

Get this thing going again

If I work alone

this thing will never end

I'm glad I've got my friends

who can help me get this

done

熊叔舌头好灵活

A good beginning makes a good ending.

善始方能善终。

对比练习

听一听，熊叔读的是哪个单词？

- get/cat
- Gee/key
- good/could

跟着熊叔大声朗读句子

- Where did you get the cat?
- Gee, I think I lost my key.
- Could you get me some good food to eat?

熊叔带你做练习

1. 很多同学喜欢玩游戏，而且在输了之后喜欢在聊天框里打"GG"，大家有没有想过"GG"是什么意思？"GG"不是哥哥，而是 good game。

2. 在外企工作的很多人都喜欢这样说话：亲爱的，我这里有一个 program，需要大家共同努力来取得巨大的progress。在这个 process 当中呢，如果有任何的 problem，请带着 solution 到我的 office 来。

3. 很多公司会要求员工在周五写周报，然后在下周一开例会汇报上一周的工作，汇报工作时常用的词汇有：

KPI（Key Performance Indicator），意为"关键绩效指标"。

OKR（Objectives and Key Results），意为"目标与关键成果法"。

KPA（Key Performance Affair），意为"关键绩效事件"。

熊叔教你唱情歌

What doesn't kill you makes you stronger

Stand a little taller

Doesn't mean I'm lonely when I'm alone

What doesn't kill you makes a fighter

Footsteps even lighter

Doesn't mean I'm over cause you're gone

What doesn't kill you makes you stronger ' stronger

Just me myself and I

What doesn't kill you makes you stronger

Stand a little taller

Doesn't mean I'm lonely when I'm alone

—*Stronger*

◎ **摩擦音：** /f/，/v/，/θ/，/ð/，/s/，/z/，/ʃ/，/ʒ/

国际音标 /f/（美式音标 /f/）

🔊 熊叔趣谈发音口型

　　首先，我们要注意不要把这个音发成汉字"夫"的发音。这是一个唇齿摩擦音，顾名思义，需要我们的嘴唇和牙齿摩擦来发音。具体做法是上齿轻轻抵住下唇内侧，然后摩擦发音，让气流从唇齿间的缝隙吹出来。

常见字母或字母组合

f — fire, fly

ff — sniff, cliff

ph — photo, phrase

gh — rough, enough

大声跟着熊叔读

lau**gh**

face

a**f**ter

英语说唱有嘻哈

You are fifty-five now and

you're still single

Party all night but you fail to mingle

You look at me like you just went through a battle

You can't be happy if you don't know how to talk to people

熊叔舌头好灵活

Fifty-five firefighters fried fifty-five French fries.

五十五名消防员油炸出五十五根炸薯条。

国际音标 /v/（美式音标 /v/）

🔊 熊叔趣谈发音口型

发此音时上齿要轻轻咬住下唇内侧，让气流从唇齿的缝隙间吹出来，此音为浊辅音，声带要跟着振动发声。一定要注意不要将 /v/ 和 /w/ 的音搞混了。

常见字母或字母组合

v — very, vase

ve — move, five

大声跟着熊叔读

a**v**oid

o**v**er

lea**v**e

dri**v**e

英语说唱有嘻哈

I just avoided running over a

cat

These cute little poor things

are not catching rats

If you love 'em, bring 'em

home and let 'em take a nap

And they'll be really happy if

you can give 'em some bags

熊叔舌头好灵活

There are rare visitors visiting

the village.

很少有游客来参观这个村庄。

对比练习

听一听，熊叔读的是哪个单词？

- very/ferry
- foot/put
- find/kind
- friend/brand

跟着熊叔大声朗读句子

- It's very cold on the ferry now.
- He put his feet in the hot water.
- Where did you find such a kind nice guy?
- My friend always tells me that I am my own brand.

熊叔带你做练习

1. 我们经常会谈到一个词——value（价值观），比如当你入职一家新公司时，你会考虑到你的 value 是否和公司的 value 相符合。那么我们所说的三观都是哪三观呢？

世界观：world view

价值观：value

人生观：outlook on life

2. 刚刚学英语的时候每个人都会说：I'm fine, thank you, and you? 但实际上这个句子用的情况并不多。它比较适合下面这样的场景。当你咳嗽时，对方问你：Are you OK? 然后你可以回答：I'm fine. 如果你感觉很好，就说：I'm doing great. / I'm very well. / Fantastic. / Excellent. 如果你感觉还行，就说：Not bad. / Fine. 如果你感觉一般，就说：Well, just so so. / I've been better. / I've been worse. 如果你感觉不好，就说：I feel terrible/awful.

3. 现在很多综艺节目都会放 VCR。在很多综艺节目中都能看到某品牌的手机代言广告。然而很多主持人都会把里面的 V 的发音发错。在这里跟熊叔学会 V 的发音，标准且地道地读出这三个字母：VCR。看美剧时经常有前情回顾：Previously…

经典美句

Every saint has a past. Every sinner has a future.

每个圣人都有过去。每个罪人也都有一个未来。

熊叔教你唱情歌

It's every little thing you do

That makes me fall in love with you

There isn't a way that I can show you

Ever since I've come to know you

It's every little thing you say

That makes me want to feel this way

There's not a thing that I can point to

Cos it's every little thing you do

—*Every Little Thing You Do*

国际音标 /θ/（美式音标 /θ/）（咬舌音）

🔊 熊叔趣谈发音口型

　　这是一个辅音，发音时用上下牙去咬自己的舌尖，放松脸部肌肉，双唇微开，让气流从牙缝里吹出来即可。我们来看这个音标的写法，中间的一横是不是就像舌头从两齿之间伸出来的样子？

常见字母或字母组合

th — thank, math

大声跟着熊叔读

thin

heal**th**y

too**th**

mo**th**

英语说唱有嘻哈

Thank you all for coming to my English class

If you behave well, I'll certainly give you a pass

Work harder, think harder, you can speak English better

Do your best and prove to me that you are a strong fighter

熊叔舌头好灵活

I thought a thought, but the thought I thought wasn't the thought I thought I thought. If the thought I thought I thought had been the thought I thought, I wouldn't have thought so much.

我有一种想法，但是我的这种想法不是我曾经想到的那种想法。如果这种想法是我曾经想到的想法，我就不会想那么多了。

国际音标 /ð/（美式音标 /ð/）

熊叔趣谈发音口型

要发准这个音，同样要微微张开双唇，咬住舌尖，但要让气流尽量被上下齿堵住，只允许少量气体逃出来，发音时声带要振动。

常见字母或字母组合

th — this, there

大声跟着熊叔读

mo<u>th</u>er

fa<u>th</u>er

bro<u>th</u>er

ba<u>the</u>

toge<u>th</u>er

英语说唱有嘻哈

Mother and father, they love me with their lives

Ever since I was little, they would hold me up so tight

Now that I'm not around them, I can only hope they're fine

One day I'mma have a big house, I'mma paint it all white

I can have dinner with my parents, and tell them both good night

(I'mma 是 I'm going to 的缩读形式。)

熊叔舌头好灵活

Whether the weather be fine or whether the weather be not, whether the weather be cold or whether the weather be hot, we'll weather the weather whether we like it or not.

无论天气是好还是坏，无论天气是冷还是热，无论我们是否喜欢，我们都将适应天气。

对比练习

听一听，熊叔读的是哪个单词？

- weather/webber
- there/hair
- this/diss
- three/free

跟着熊叔大声朗读句子

- And Webber said, "how's the weather？"
- Uncle Bear's wife yelled at him, "whose hair is it?"
- This is not cool, bro. You don't have the courage to diss me.
- Let's set these three ducks free.

熊叔带你做练习

  1. 用咬舌音说的最多的词有 this、that。如果你在国外的餐厅点餐，一时语塞，也可以指着菜单说："I want this, I want that, thank you."

  2. 如果你见到老外一时间不知道说什么好，可以讨论 weather。比如：

The weather's great here in Miami! I love it!

3. 关于"谢谢",还可以用以下不同的说法来表达:

Thanks a million.

Thanks for everything.

Thank you for doing…

I can't thank you enough.

4. Learning without thought is labor lost; thought without learning is perilous.

学而不思则罔,思而不学则殆。

is he cute or what

经典美句

When someone sees you at your worst and still thinks you look your best, that is someone worth keeping.

值得你留住的人是即使看到你最糟糕的一面，依然认为你很美的人。

熊叔教你唱情歌

Beautiful girls all over the world, I could be chasing

But my time would be wasted, they got nothing on you, baby

Nothing on you, baby

They might say hi, and I might say hey

But you shouldn't worry, about what they say

Because they got nothing on you, baby

Nothing on you, baby

[Verse 1- B.o.B]

I know you feel where I'm coming from

Regardless of the things in my past that I've done

Most of it really was for the hell of the fun

On a carousel, so around I spun

With no direction, just trying to get some

Trying to chase skirts, living in the summer sun

And so I lost more than I had ever won

And honestly, I ended up with none

—Nothing On You

国际音标 /s/（美式音标 /s/）

🔊 熊叔趣谈发音口型

　　这个音还是很容易发的。它看上去有点像一条贪吃蛇。如果你不小心踩了一条蛇的尾巴，那么蛇会对你发出"s"的声音。发音时舌头中部拱起贴近上颚，舌尖靠近下齿龈，舌头两边分别抵住两边的上牙，好像你在舌头下面藏了什么东西一样。嘴巴变小，气流通过，声带不发出声音。

常见字母或字母组合

s — school, sunny

ss — boss, press

c — agency, cancel

大声跟着熊叔读

li**s**ten

stay

英语说唱有嘻哈

Drive around all alone on the freeway

Listening to the rhythm of the falling rain

My brain wants me to drive far
far away
But my heart is telling me for
her I should stay

熊叔舌头好灵活

In the passage the passenger
passed a cassette of message
to messenger.
在过道里，乘客给信差传递了
一盒录有信息的磁带。

国际音标 /z/（美式音标 /z/）

🔊 熊叔趣谈发音口型

　　把 /s/ 音浊化，声带振动便可以发出 /z/ 音。注意 /z/ 音如果在
单词词尾的话，一般会发得很轻，不会完整地发出来。

常见字母或字母组合

z — zoo, citizen
s — easy, as

大声跟着熊叔读

ea<u>s</u>y
do<u>z</u>e
ja<u>zz</u>

英语说唱有嘻哈

I just want to doze for a while
Listen to Jazz for a while
Play my guitar for a while
Think about nothing for a
while
Cuz I've been working too
much, worrying too much

But I don't get enough sleep

Even though I've counted sheep

熊叔舌头好灵活

I am amazed it is a craze these days to dance to music of Jazz.

这些疯狂地随着爵士乐起舞的日子对我来说太棒了。

对比练习

听一听，熊叔读的是哪个单词?

- think/sink
- zoos/those
- nice/ninth
- does/dust

跟着熊叔大声朗读句子

- I think the boat is sinking.
- How many zoos arc there?
- My boy was the ninth in the race.
- Look at the dust on his books. Does he read at all?

熊叔带你做练习

大家应该都认识 easy 这个词，但是你知道它的诸多用法吗？

easy 最常见的释义为"容易的、简单的"，其反义词是 difficult，意为"困难的"。这里提到反义词是因为很多同学容易混淆 easy 和 simple 的释义。simple 的反义词是 complicated，意为"复杂的"，通过各自的反义词就可以轻松地将这两个词区分开了，easy 表示"不难的那种简单"，simple 表示"不复杂的那种简易"。接下来，我们来看看 easy 常见的使用场景：

· "Easy!"可以直接单独使用，表示"淡定！""冷静！""放松点！"比如，你看到别人在打架，有人试图动用利器去伤人，这时你可以去阻止他并对他说："Easy！"

· "Take it easy！"可以用的场合非常多，表示"别紧张""别着急""别放在心上""放轻松"等。比如，当别人要发火时，你可以安抚他说："Take it easy!"再如，看到别人很紧张时，你也可以对他说："Take it easy!"

· Go easy on something，表示"省着点""少用点"等。比如，好朋友们在一起聚餐，忍不住要多喝几杯酒，有的人已经酩酊大醉，却还要继续喝，这时我们便可以对他说："Go easy on the alcohol!"

· Go easy on someone 也可以用来表示"对某人温和

点"。比如，你和你的好朋友吵架，你的好朋友很凶又不听你说话，那你就可以对他说："Can you go easy on me?"

- Easy for you to say，表示"你说得容易"。比如，你和你好朋友吵架时，你对他说："Can you go easy on me?"这时，对方便可以对你说："Easy for you to say!"言下之意就是，"你说得容易，你那么气人我凭什么对你温柔！"

经典美句

Life is simple, you make a choice and don't look back.

生活是简单的，你做出了选择，就不要回头。

熊叔教你唱情歌

The wine and the lights and the Spanish guitar

I'll never forget how romantic they are

But I know, tomorrow I'll lose the one I love

There's no way to come with you（way to come with you）

It's the only thing to do

Oh

Just one last dance（Oh）

Before we say goodbye（say goodbye）

When we sway and turn around and round and round

It's like the first time

Just one more chance

Hold me tight and keep me warm（keep me warm）

Cause the night is getting cold

And I don't know where I belong

—Just One Last Dance

国际音标 /ʃ/（美式音标 /ʃ/）

🔊 熊叔趣谈发音口型

　　我们先来读一小段汉语的绕口令：四是四，十是十，十四是十四，四十是四十。如果你发音时分不出"四"和"十"，那你很可能也读不准 /ʃ/ 这个英文音标。尽管熊叔在前面一再强调要忘记汉语发音去学音标，但是不得不承认的是，说汉语时平翘舌不分的同学大部分学英语时也发不准 /s/ 或 /ʃ/。

　　发 /ʃ/ 音时，我们要把舌头抬起来。设想情景，你刚吃完一块特别硬的牛排，左边的上牙缝（内侧）和右边的上牙缝（内侧）塞满了牛肉渣，你想用舌头把它们弄出来。这时你的口型便与发此音的口型相似。发音时，使舌尖保持上翘，嘴巴略上翘，气流通过，发出 /ʃ/ 音。

　　发 /ʃ/ 音和 /s/ 音最大的区别是舌尖的位置。发 /s/ 时舌尖在下齿龈附近，发 /ʃ/ 音时舌尖则是上翘，处于靠近上颌的位置。

常见字母或字母组合

s —— sugar, sure

sh —— ash, brush

ch —— machine, chef

大声跟着熊叔读

ru**sh**

shop

英语说唱有嘻哈

It's almost midnight here on November 11th

Everybody is shopping online with their cellphones
Wives are trying to get their shopping cart done
While husbands are looking at their money run

熊叔舌头好灵活

An English fisherman wishes to get a foolish fish for a cold dish.
一个英国的渔夫希望捕到一条自投罗网的鱼来充饥。

国际音标 /ʒ/（美式音标 /ʒ/）

🔊 熊叔趣谈发音口型

这是一个很难发出的辅音，因为这个声音很难模仿。但实际上，只要我们了解发音时的口型，就不难发了。发 /ʒ/ 音时的口型和发 /ʃ/ 音时的口型是一模一样的。区别在于发 /ʒ/ 音时振动声带。

常见字母或字母组合

s — usually, decision

g — garage, regime

大声跟着熊叔读

mea**s**ure

u**s**ual

plea**s**ure

英语说唱有嘻哈

Now the pain is my pleasure, nothing can measure

New rules for her. Me? She can't hurt

Don't pick up the phone, don't tell her where you were

She's gonna break you yet again, in case you haven't heard

熊叔舌头好灵活

I can't endure the leisure man's measure for the treasures in the treasury.

我不能容忍那个悠闲男子对金库里的财宝所采取的措施。

对比练习

听一听，熊叔读的是哪个单词?

- sob/shop
- sue/shoe
- sure/sore
- usual/user

跟着熊叔大声朗读句子

- Hey, don't sob, let's go shopping together!
- He got sued because he didn't wear any shoes in his office.
- Are you sure you want to go to Disneyland? Your feet are going to feel very sore.
- As usual, users pay $10 to download the video.

熊叔带你做练习

　　1. 工作中经常会用到电子表格，里面的工作表 sheet 想必大家都非常熟悉。可是总有人把"sheet"发成"西 t"或者"施 t"，这就是将用汉语发音技巧用在英语发音中的结果。

2. 我们在日常生活中最常做的两件事：go to the supermarket 和 go shopping。supermarket 是 s 开头，而 shopping 是 sh 开头，注意要区分开这两处的发音。

3. 如果你说汉语时就平翘舌不分，那么要区分开 s 和 sh 的发音可能要进一步进行训练。记住，发 s 音时，舌尖是处在下齿龈处的，舌头中部向上顶住上颚。而发 sh 音时，请大家先保持 s 的口型不动，然后把舌尖抬起来上翘，抬起来的同时，舌头中部顶住上颚的部分会自然下落，而舌头左右两侧抵住上牙的左右两侧。

经典美句

When I'm shouting, I'm fine. But when I go silent you need to be worried.

当我还能大吵大闹的时候，其实我没事。但是如果我沉默不语的话，你就要担心了。

熊叔教你唱情歌

This is ten percent luck

Twenty percent skill

Fifteen percent concentrated power of will

Five percent pleasure

Fifty percent pain

And a hundred percent reason to remember the name

—*Remember the Name*

◎ 破擦音：/tʃ/，/dʒ/，/tr/，/dr/，/ts/，/dz/

还记得之前熊叔练过的 beatbox 吗？我们来给它升个级：
boots, chats, boom, boom, chats, butcher, butcher, bobo, true, true.

国际音标 /tʃ/ （美式音标 /tʃ/）

◀)) **熊叔趣谈发音口型**

我们可以将 /tʃ/ 音理解为把 /t/ 和 /ʃ/ 组合在了一起。那我们在发音的时候，先做出 /ʃ/ 的口型来，然后再把舌尖抬起来，顶住上颚，保持不动，现在嘴里的气流会被堵住。然后瞬间使气流冲出，嘴巴向外吐气，双唇可以略微向外凸出，发出 /tʃ/ 音。注意声带不要发出声音。

常见字母或字母组合

ch — church, chat

tch — butcher, kitchen

t — question, nature

大声跟着熊叔读

check

tea**ch**

wat**ch**

英语说唱有嘻哈

Hey, yo, check it out, this video is dope

The master is teaching the dog to say nope

Been watching this for an

hour, and I miss the show

The weekend is almost over, and I haven't done anything at all

Don't you laugh at me, cuz you're just the same as me

Take a look at yourself in the mirror, and tell me what you see

熊叔舌头好灵活

The chief chief chewed the cheap cheese.

首席长官嚼着便宜的奶酪。

🐧 国际音标 /dʒ/（美式音标 /dʒ/）

🔊 熊叔趣谈发音口型

/dʒ/ 与 /tʃ/ 的发音口型相似，把 /tʃ/ 音浊化，声带振动。

常见字母或字母组合

j — jump, jazz

g — general, gentle

dg — budget, lodger

大声跟着熊叔读

join

just

英语说唱有嘻哈

Just get off work, I'm heading to the party

And if you feel like it, you can come and join me

I've got a friend coming over, and she looks really pretty

Maybe you can be together, maybe it's destiny

熊叔舌头好灵活

In the exchange the oranges are arranged into strange ranges.

在交易所里，橙子被奇怪地排成了几排。

对比练习

听一听，熊叔读的是哪个单词？

- teach/tease
- job/sob
- shop/chop

跟着熊叔大声朗读句子

- The teacher got fired for teasing his students.
- Sobbing isn't going to get you a job.
- Chop, chop! Let's go shopping!

熊叔带你做练习

　　同学们在大学毕业的时候会面临找工作的问题，熊叔在这里给大家介绍一些跟找工作相关的用语和表达：

　　"找工作"最口语化的表达是 get a job、look for a job、apply for a job 等，比较书面的名词是 job-hunting。当你去面试时，你是 interviewee，面试你的面试官是 interviewer。当你被聘用了，你会收到 offer，成为 employee，雇用你的人或公司是 employer。

　　如果你还没毕业，会有个 internship（实习期）。如果你已经毕业了，会有个 probation（试用期）。如果你工作做得不错，会 get a promotion（升职）、get a raise（加薪）。如果你工作做得不好，被辞退了，可以说 get fired，get sacked，be dismissed 或者简单地说 kick… out。被炒了之后，你便 unemployed（失业了）。工作类型可分为两种：一种是 a part-time job（一份兼职工作）；另一种是 a full-time job（一份全职工作）。最近几年还开始流行 SOHO（Small Office/Home Office）的模式，意为"在家办公"。

经典美句

Life doesn't just happen to you, you receive everything in your life based on what you've given.

你身上发生的一切都不是偶然，你从生活里得到了什么，源于你给予了什么。

国际音标 /tr/（美式音标 /tr/）

🔊 熊叔趣谈发音口型

注意不要将这个音发成汉字"戳"的音。这个音是结合了 /t/ 和 /r/ 的发音，但是要比发 /r/ 音更容易一些。我们先摆好 /t/ 的口型，然后舌头上部收拢上翘，舌身呈凹形，双唇稍稍噘起，送气的同时，舌头上部向嘴里面的方向回收。注意声带不要发出声音。

常见字母或字母组合

tr — try, trip

大声跟着熊叔读

travel

trip

frus**tr**ated

英语说唱有嘻哈

When you feel frustrated and lost, ask for a week off from your boss

Take a trip by the beach and relax

Lie in the sand and have some snacks

Sometime you feel you got smacked
Traveling can heal all the cracked

熊叔舌头好灵活

Never trouble about trouble until trouble troubles you.
不要自找麻烦。

国际音标 /dr/（美式音标 /dr/）

🔊 熊叔趣谈发音口型

　　注意不要将这个音发成汉字"捉"的音，它与 /tr/ 的发音口型相似，把 /tr/ 音浊化，声带发出声音，便发出 /dr/ 音来。

常见字母或字母组合

dr — drop, dress

大声跟着熊叔读

dream
drive
drunk
drug

英语说唱有嘻哈

Last night I had a dream, I was drunk and alone
I was driving on the street with nothing but a phone
I was disappointed that the phone never rang
But suddenly, out of nowhere, the ringtone sang
Lasl thing I remembered was a crash with a bang
The street was blocked, I was taken out of the Mustang

The car I hit, there was a baby in it

God, I wish you had taken me instead of two-year-old kid

When I woke up the next morning, I was covered in sweat

I got a hangover, I wasn't

driving, and no one was dead

熊叔舌头好灵活

The drummer drummed and he dreamed to be a great drummer.

这位鼓手在敲鼓，他梦想成为一名伟大的鼓手。

对比练习

听一听，熊叔读的是哪个单词?

- dream/trim
- tree/three
- cheat/treat
- drag/Jack

跟着熊叔大声朗读句子

- I had a dream last night. I was trimming in my dream.
- There're three trees in my yard. I was kidding. I don't even

have a house.

- You've been treating her really well after she cheated on you.
- Jack dragged me to a bar. He said his wife cheated on him.

熊叔带你做练习

驾照：driver's license

自驾游：self-driving tour / road trip

跟团游：package tour

自助游：DIY tour / self-guided tour

深度游：in-depth tour

主题游：theme tour

徒步游：go hiking

观光游览：go sightseeing

度假：go on a vacation

经典美句

Try to be a rainbow in someone's cloud.

当有人身处阴霾之下时，尽力去做他们的"彩虹"。

熊叔教你唱情歌

Ever wonder 'bout what he's doing

How it's all turned to lies

Sometimes I think that it's better

To never ask why

Where there is desire, there is gonna be a flame

Where there is a flame, someone's bound to get burned

But just because it burns, doesn't mean you're gonna die

You gotta get up and try, and try, and try

Gotta get up and try, and try, and try

You gotta get up and try, and try, and try

—*Try*

国际音标 /ts/（美式音标 /ts/）

🔊 熊叔趣谈发音口型

这个音是 /t/ 和 /s/ 的组合音（美式发音）。在国外的一些学者看来，这个音甚至不构成一个单独的音标，只是两个音组合到了一起而已。我们可以尝试把两个音快速地发出来，进而使其成为一个音。这个音发音时从 /t/ 音的口型开始，发音时舌尖向下，要注意，仅仅是舌尖向下，舌身保持不动，从而发出 /ts/ 音。

常见字母或字母组合

ts — lots, cats

大声跟着熊叔读

lo**ts**

ca**ts**

英语说唱有嘻哈

I was driving along the street when I saw lots of cats

All of them were starving except for one that was fat

I pitied the skinny ones so I put them in some bags

And I carried them home and fed them really tasty snacks

But I ran out of cat food just two days from that

And the cats were pooping everywhere which really drove me mad

熊叔舌头好灵活

I packed the jackets and rackets into packets with sacks.

我用袋子将夹克衫和球拍打成小包。

国际音标 /dz/（美式音标 /dz/）

🔊 熊叔趣谈发音口型

　　/dz/ 与 /ts/ 的发音口型相似，也是两个辅音的组合音，有时也不被算作独立的音标。注意这个音和 /z/ 音听着很像，但是发音时的口型是不同的。/dz/ 音是从发 /d/ 音开始的，发音时舌尖向下动，发音过程中舌身前段仍然上拱。而发 /z/ 音时，舌头比较懒，在发音时舌尖一直在下齿龈处平放不动。/dz/ 和 /ts/ 往往出现在名词复数或者动词第三人称单数的形式中。

常见字母或字母组合

ds — han**ds**, be**ds**

大声跟着熊叔读

see**ds**

san**ds**

frien**ds**

min**ds**

han**ds**

英语说唱有嘻哈

I've made some new friends, together we join hands

Go to the beaches, make a fort on the sands

Staring at the sea and sky so high

We're dropping all the troubles and the chores off our minds

熊叔舌头好灵活

He puts his hands into the beds to look for the cards and codes.

他把手伸进床里想找到卡片和密码。

对比练习

听一听，熊叔读的是哪个单词？

* writes/rice

* cars/cards

* sees/seeds

跟着熊叔大声朗读句子

* The poor writer writes something about rice.

* He's got twelve fancy cars, while I've got two transportation cards.

* In spring, you bury seeds. In fall, you'll harvest fruits.

熊叔带你做练习

debit card：借记卡

credit card：信用卡

VISA/MASTER card：（可以在国外消费的）信用卡

platinum card：（需要一定消费水平的）白金卡

ID card：身份证

passport：护照

sim card：手机卡

business card：名片

transportation card：交通卡

经典美句

The opening credits began, lighting the room by a token amount. My eyes, of their own accord, flickered to him.

片头字幕开始了，微弱的光线象征性地照亮屋子。我的眼睛，出于它们自己的意愿，飞快地向他一瞥。

熊叔教你唱情歌

This world so trife

Your money or your life

Yeah keep your kids

Keep your wife

Money or your life

Give it up

This world so trife

So trife

Your money or your life

West Coast

Yeah keep your kids

Keep your wife

Money or your life

—Your Money or Your Life

◎ 鼻音：/m/，/n/，/ŋ/

英语中的鼻音是相对比较重的音，我们在感冒的时候可以找找鼻腔发声的感觉，或者也可以拱起鼻子去模仿牛叫。当你能自由地运用鼻腔发声的时候，读准下面这几个鼻音也就非常简单了。

注意：母语中前后鼻音不分的同学请把这里的鼻音学 5 遍以上。

国际音标 /m/（美式音标 /m/）

熊叔趣谈发音口型

强烈建议大家在学这个音之前去听一听 Lady Gaga 的歌曲 *Poker Face*，前面的一串"muh muh muh muh..."发这个"muh"音时能让你瞬间找到发 /m/ 音的感觉。发 /m/ 音时，双唇要紧闭，舌头要放平，声带振动发声，让气流从鼻孔排出。

常见字母或字母组合

m — mother, much

mm — common, summer

大声跟着熊叔读

Mike

milk

men

meet

make

英语说唱有嘻哈

Once there was a rapper named Mike

He really wanted to be heard through his mic

He felt so different and that his raps were unlike

His haters and he thought he was one of a kind

He made a living from rapping and he tried to make his ends meet so that he could focus his mind on something that he really liked and he didn't have to leave his career behind

And that's what he does now, a rapper redefined

Are you living the life you want even though it's rather fine

熊叔舌头好灵活

I scream, you scream, we all scream for ice-cream.

我喊，你喊，我们都喊着要冰淇淋。

国际音标 /n/（美式音标 /n/）

🔊 熊叔趣谈发音口型

练这个音之前，先深深地用鼻子哼一口气，感受鼻腔振动的感觉。发这个音时的口型和发 /t/ 音时非常像，摆好 /t/ 的口型，舌尖抵住上齿龈，声带振动，鼻腔振动，发出 /n/ 的音。当你发完这个音后，舌尖自然下垂，会带出一个小尾音来，这也是正常的。这里建议大家一定要观看熊叔的视频来仔细体会。

常见字母或字母组合

n — north, number

nn — funny, manner

大声跟着熊叔读

o**n**

rui**n**

ow**n**

英语说唱有嘻哈

There's a ring on her finger

You've gotta stop thinking about her

She's got a perfect marriage for years

You wouldn't ruin that if you really loved her

Maybe you don't really love her

Maybe you just want to own her

She's not an object you can claim yours

You're just a twisted weird admirer

熊叔舌头好灵活

You know that I know that you know. I know that you know | that I know.
你知道我知道你知道的。我知道你知道我知道的。

国际音标 /ŋ/（美式音标 /ŋ/）

🔊 **熊叔趣谈发音口型**

熊叔把这个音称为"大鼻音"。这个音很难发，发着也很累，有时候外国人也懒得发完整。发 /n/ 音时舌尖上翘，舔上齿龈，而发 /ŋ/ 音时舌身中部拱起，抵住上颚，舌身前部、舌尖自然下垂，声带振动，发出 /ŋ/ 音来。

常见字母或字母组合

n — link, pink
ng — raining, sing

大声跟着熊叔读

ri**ng**
runni**ng**
comi**ng**
sleepi**ng**

英语说唱有嘻哈

Uncle Bear asked me to sing you a song

I'm telling you I can do it all night long

I want to protect you just like King Kong

Together, I'll love you forever

We could be stronger

Our life could be better

熊叔舌头好灵活

The spring brings many charming things.

春天带来了很多迷人的东西。

对比练习

听一听，熊叔读的是哪个单词？

- thin/thing
- rings/rinse
- sing/sin
- think/thick

跟着熊叔大声朗读句子

- This thing can make you thin.
- If you want it then you've got to put a ring on it.
- Can Uncle Bear sing?
- Do you think the wall is thick and strong enough to weather the storm?

熊叔带你做练习

　　熊叔接触过上百万名学员，打招呼基本上是清一色的
"How are you" "Fine, thank you" "And you"，无论想要
表达怎样的心情都只会用这一句话。伤心失恋了回复："I'm
fine, thank you. And you?" 在上海排了两年牌照终于排到了
也回复："I'm fine, thank you. And you?" 不懂英语的同学或
许觉得这句话是比较万能的。其实，fine 一般表示"健康的
状态"。比如，熊叔刚打了两个喷嚏还咳嗽了两声，你过来表
示关心，问："Are you OK?" 这时候我才会说："Fine, thank
you." (我没事儿，谢谢。) 电视剧《老友记》中 Ross 离婚后
朋友问起她的状况时，她回答的也是："I'll be fine."

　　那么，怎样才是更地道的打招呼呢？美国人其实更喜欢
用"How are you doing?" 口语中往往简化成"How're ya
doin'?" 大鼻音简化成了 /n/。回答可以是：

I'm doing great.

I'm doing fine.

I'm doing very well.

在这里，熊叔给大家介绍几个打招呼必备的句子。

How are you doing？最近怎么样？

How's it going? 最近怎么样？

How's everything at home/work? 家里 / 工作一切都好吗？

What's up? 最近怎么样？

What's new? 有什么新鲜事？

I'm doing well/great. 我很好。

Same as usual. 老样子。

Nothing special. 没什么特别的。

I haven't seen you for ages. 好久不见你了!

What have you been up to? 你最近在忙什么?

It's good to see you again. 再见到你真是太好了。

经典美句

The grain, which is also golden, will bring me back the thought of you. And I shall love to listen to the wind in the wheat...
小麦也是金黄色的,那会使我想起你。我会喜欢听麦田里的风声……

熊叔教你唱情歌

It starts with one thing

I don't know why

It doesn't even matter

How hard you try

Keep that in mind

I designed this rhyme

To explain in due time

All I know

Time is a valuable thing

Watch it fly by

As the pendulum swings

Watch it count down

To the end of the day

The clock ticks life away

It's so unreal

—In The End

◎ 舌边音 /l/ 及其他摩擦音：/r/，/h/

国际音标 /l/（美式音标 /l/）

◀》熊叔趣谈发音口型

这个音有两种发音情况：

1. 当此音位于元音前时，我们把舌尖舔到上齿龈，然后把舌头从上齿龈的地方向下移，其间声带振动，移动的瞬间发出这个音。比如，"like""love"的发音。

2. 当此音为尾音时，舌尖舔在上齿龈发声就可以了，不要移下来。注意舌尖一定要翘起来，抵住上齿龈，如"fall"中的发音。

3. 很多时候这个音会和其他的辅音如 /b/、/t/、/d/ 等构成一个单独的音节，两个辅音贴在一起。比如，little、dribble、huddle 等。这个音节在词典里有时直接显示为 /bl/、/tl/、/dl/，有时也会写成 /bəl/、/təl/、/dəl/，大家见到的时候知道这是其中的一个辅音和 /l/ 组成的单独的音节就可以了。

　　4. 上述规则中，/k/ 和 /l/ 组合在一起时容易和 /əʊ/(/o/) 的音搞混。我们来比较一下 cycle 和 psycho 的发音。cycle 在发音的时候，明显在发最后的尾音 /l/ 时舌尖处于上齿龈处顶着，而 psycho 在发最后的尾音时，舌头是平放在口腔内的，明显区别于前者。

常见字母或字母组合

l — last, long

ll — yellow, allow

大声跟着熊叔读

look

lunch

life

ill

live

little

英语说唱有嘻哈

Hey girl, look at me, don't worry

about the bill

You've got a cold, and it's fine, everyone gets ill

Remember, there's a cure, just relax and chill

You'll be all right in just a week, and you've got your dreams to fulfill

熊叔舌头好灵活

A little pill may well cure a great ill.

一粒小药丸可能治愈大疾病。

国际音标 /r/（美式音标 /r/）

🔊 熊叔趣谈发音口型

这个就是传说中的卷舌音了。不过我们只是把它叫作卷舌音或者儿化音。发此音时，双唇张开且稍向前突出，舌尖上扬即可，不用非要卷到最里面去。气流从舌面上方流出，舌头向下，同时振动声带发声。

常见字母或字母组合

r — right, rice

rr — arrest, error

rh — rhino, rhythm

wr — wrong, wrestle

大声跟着熊叔读

ve**r**y

mise**r**able

f**r**eestyle

wrinkle

英语说唱有嘻哈

A girl from my class asked me if I was free

If I didn't get it wrong the girl got something for me

So, I said yeah, I'm up all week

She said, "I like your brother, can you introduce him for me?"

熊叔舌头好灵活

The boundary around the round ground separates us from the surroundings.

围绕着圆形场地的边界将我们和周围的环境隔开。

国际音标 /h/（美式音标 /h/）

熊叔趣谈发音口型

发 /h/ 音时，只要稍微张开嘴巴，使气息通过且向外呵气，就可发出此音。从喉咙深处让这口气轻轻呵出即可，不需要振动声带发声。

常见字母或字母组合

h — his, house
wh — whom, who

大声跟着熊叔读

hard-**h**earted
hunter
hunt
hare

英语说唱有嘻哈

I was in the woods when I saw the hard-hearted hunter
He came here with only one goal, it was to hunt for fur
Hares, bears, even lions and tigers
He shot everything and everything moved farther
I was so afraid that my world was almost a blur
I lied down in the bushes until the sky got darker
I wasn't exposed but I was certainly not a fighter
In a dark forest like this, survival comes first
You can never be too careful with the forest ruler

熊叔舌头好灵活

The hunter and his huge horse hide behind the house.
猎人和他的大马藏在房子后面。

109

对比练习

听一听，熊叔读的是哪个单词？

- light/night/right

- heard/nerd

- wrong/long

- love/rough

跟着熊叔大声朗读句子

- It's midnight, with the lights out. But you're still awake, right?

- I heard the nerd singing in his room. Terrible.

- Uncle Bear has long hair? Feels so wrong.

- His hands were rough because he worked too much.

熊叔带你做练习

这里熊叔给大家分享一些浪漫的英文句子：

1. "Do you have a map? Because, I just got lost in your eyes."

请问你有地图吗？因为我已经迷失在你的眼眸里了。

2. "Can I have your phone number? Because I lost mine."

你能告诉我你的电话号码吗？我忘了自己的号码。

3. "What's your sign? Seems like we're a perfect match."

你是什么星座的？我们似乎是完美的一对。

4. "There are three things I want to do before I die and you're fulfilling one of them."

在我死前我有三件事必须完成，你就是其中一件。

5. "I must be in heaven, because you're an angel."

我现在一定是在天堂，因为你是一位天使。

经典美句

Meeting you was fate and falling in love with you was out of my control.

遇见你是命运的安排，而爱上你是我情不自禁。

熊叔教你唱情歌

Almost heaven west virginia

Blue ridge mountains shenandoah river

Life is old there older than the trees

Younger than the mountains

Growing like a breeze

Country roads take me home

To the place I belong

West virginia

Mountain momma

Take me home country roads

—Take Me Home Country Road

◎ 半元音：/w/，/j/

国际音标 /w/（美式音标 /w/）

🔊 熊叔趣谈发音口型

所谓半元音就是一半发音像元音，介于元音和辅音之间，从辅助口型滑动而形成的音。发 /w/ 音时，舌后部抬高，双唇收圆，自由吐气，然后双唇自然张开，声带需要振动发声。通常半元音会和元音连接，形成一个过渡的口型。

常见字母或字母组合

w — wind, wig

wh — when, why（注意美式发音当中，字母组合 wh 发 /w/ 的时候，前面往往会加一个很轻的 /h/ 的音，发成 /hw/。比如，when 会发成 /hwɛn/）

大声跟着熊叔读

when

work

will

where

way

英语说唱有嘻哈

When a man loves a woman, he gives her all his heart

He works like he's in prison, his life is getting hard

He wishes to have a garden, he wishes to have a **y**ard

The apartment they're renting is so cramped and they can see the stars

113

熊叔舌头好灵活

A snow-white swan swam swiftly to catch a slowly-swimming snake in a lake.

湖里的一只雪白的天鹅快速地游动着去追赶一条正在缓慢游动着的蛇。

国际音标 /j/（美式音标 /j/）

🔊 熊叔趣谈发音口型

发 /j/ 音时的口型起点接近于发 /i/ 时的口型，摆好发 /i/ 音的口型之后，气流自由呼出，嘴巴自然放松，舌头中部由高到低滑动，声带需要振动发声。

常见字母或字母组合

y — yell, year

大声跟着熊叔读

yell
yawn
yoga
yard

英语说唱有嘻哈

Stop yelling stop whining everything will be fine
You're only 20, but look at your hairline
Relax yourself and you've got to make your worries resign
Nothing's a big deal, help yourself to a glass of wine

熊叔舌头好灵活

The yellow bird has yelled for many years in the yard of | Yale.

那只黄鸟在耶鲁大学的校园里唱歌已经有好多年了。

对比练习

听一听，熊叔读的是哪个单词？

- yeah/ear
- weird/wired
- where/hair

跟着熊叔大声朗读句子

- Remember, walls have ears, yeah?
- It's weird. You are weird. Everybody is so weird around here.
- Uncle Bear, where's your hair?

熊叔带你做练习

Yes 在口语中有很多种变体，每个变体又可以表示多种含义，我们一起来看看吧。

Yes，意为"是"。升调的时候可以表示"什么事儿"；降调的时候除了表示肯定之外，也可以表示兴奋的情绪等。

Yeah，升调的时候可以表示"什么""怎么了"；降调的时候可以表示"是呀""好呀"；加入特殊的语气时也可以表示无奈、恍然大悟等。有时候，说话人也可以故意拖长单词的前半部分发音来表达特定的情绪。

Yep，有些调皮的感觉，说的时候一般比较轻快。

经典美句

I hope you realize that you trying to keep your distance from me in no way lessens my affection for you. All your efforts to keep me from you are gonna fail.

我希望你明白，即使你跟我保持距离，我对你的深情也丝毫不减。一切试图让我远离你的努力都将是徒劳的。

熊叔教你唱情歌

What do you mean? Ooh

When you nod your head yes

But you wanna say no

What do you mean? Hey

When you don't want me to move

But you tell me to go

What do you mean

Oh, what do you mean

Said we're running out of time

What do you mean

Oh oh oh what do you mean

Better make up your mind

What do you mean

—*What Do You Mean*

2

容易混淆的
音标对比训练

熊叔在本章中列出了 14 组比较容易混淆音标发音的单词，来帮助大家做区分练习。

关注微信公众号"熊叔英语"，回复"音标对比训练"，收听熊叔真人示范发音！

一、seat VS sit

- Have a seat, please. 请坐。
- Sit down, please. 请坐。

两个单词的发音不仅仅是"长短"的区别，甚至在美音音标中，都是没有长音符号的。中国学生一般非常擅长发 seat 这个所谓的"长音"，但实际上，根据我们前面所学的内容，seat 和 sit 的发音在口型上是有较大的区别的。我们先发 seat 的音，保持住 sea 这部分的口型，然后把嘴巴张开一点，使口腔内部空间更大一点，然后发出 sit。我们可以这样记，seat、sit、set、sat 这些词的口型是依次逐渐由小变大的，那么 sit 的口型大小应该在 seat 和 set 之间，这样就容易区分了。

二、bed VS bad

- This bed looks nice. 这张床看上去挺漂亮的。
- You are a bad boy. 你是个坏小子。

在前面讲到的 seat 和 sit 的发音对比当中，熊叔强调了 seat、sit、set、sat 发音时的口型依次是由小到大的，那么同理 bed 发音时的口型肯定要比 bad 小，介于 bad 和 bid 之间。当你还是区分不开时，熊叔还有一个妙招来帮助你区分 bed 和 bad。你先假装跟别人打招呼，说"嘿，你好啊"，在说"嘿"的时候停住，保持这时的口型大小，然后按照 /ε/ 的发音方式去发音，舌头中部向下，口腔内部稍微紧张一些。接下来假装自己在大笑，张大嘴巴发"哈哈哈"，然后在"哈"的基础上，嘴唇收紧，舌头中后部微微抬起，发出 bad 音。我们可以再试着读 bead、bid、bed、bad 这四个单词来感受口型的变化。

三、Luke VS look

- Luke, this shirt is for you. 卢克，这件衬衫是给你的。
- Look! This shirt is for you! 看！这件衬衫是给你的！

这两个单词发音的区别不仅仅在于音标的长短。当我们在发"Luke"这个所谓的长音时，口型会缩得很小，嘴唇收紧，嘴巴微微噘起来，口腔内部也要收紧；而"look"这个所谓的短元音，则是在发 Luke 音的基础上，把嘴唇放开，口腔内部也要稍稍放开一些。在美剧《摩登家庭》中，以西班牙语为母语的 Gloria 就经常分不清这些发音，而正好有一个角色的名字叫 Luke，所以她有时候分不清别人是在叫"Luke"还是在让她"look"，别人有时候也分不清 Gloria 到底是在喊"Luke"还是在叫别人"look"。

四、see VS thief

- I see a thief on the street. 我在街上看到一个小偷。
- The thief I see is Uncle Bear! 我看见的那个小偷是熊叔！

这里主要比较的是 /s/ 音和咬舌音 /θ/。母语是汉语的我们，刚开始听到这两个单词的发音时会感到很难区分，但是我们可以记住一句话：能说出来的，就肯定能听得懂。所以我们在区分这两个音时，一定要知道它们所对应的发音口型。发音时，咬舌音 /θ/ 的口型和 /s/ 的口型相差比较大。发 /θ/ 音时舌尖在两齿之间，使气流通过而发出。口型上的差异，能让你轻松地区分二者的发音，只要你能读准，慢慢就能听出它们的区别了。

有类似发音的单词还有 fourth 和 force。电影《星球大战》里有一句经典的台词：May the force be with you（希望原力与你同在）。如果 force 和 fourth 分不清，那就成了"May the fourth be with you"，则意为："愿五四青年节与你同在。"

五、see VS she

- She sees me. 她看到了我。
- She can see Uncle Bear. 她能看到熊叔。

这两个单词发音的区别类似于汉语中的平翘舌的区别。要区分自己容易混淆的音，最好的办法就是先发其中的一个音，然后由这个音的口型直接转变到发另外一个音的口型，从而清晰地感受两者发音时口型的区别。比如，区别 see 和 she 的发音，我们就先发 see，/s/ 音大家都比较熟悉，舌尖在下，舌头中后部上翘，和上颚形成空间，摩擦出音。然后保持发 /s/ 音时的口型不动，随后我们直接转变成发 /ʃ/ 音。发 /s/ 音后，把舌尖上翘，同时舌头中部会塌陷下去，舌头两侧抵住上牙两侧，这样让舌尖和上齿龈后面形成一个空间，气流从那里出来。记住，我们一定要记住每个音发音时的口型，不要仅靠模仿声音来读单词。

六、load VS road VS note

- You don't know? She's loaded! 你不知道吗？她非常有钱！
- Check your note on the road. 在路上看你的笔记吧。

这一组单词的发音，我们先来看 /l/ 音，在学音标的时候熊叔已经强调过，/l/ 音的发音要点就是让舌尖舔到上齿龈，然后舌尖向下抖出这个音来。接下来，保持 /l/ 的口型，我们加入鼻音，鼻子全程有被"拎"起来的感觉，这时便发出 /n/ 音来。当 /l/ 在元音前时，和 /n/ 的发音差别基本上就在于鼻腔发不发声。我们再次保持 /l/ 的口型，把嘴唇收紧，舌尖离开上齿龈再向上卷起，到差不多垂直上颚的角度，压缩一下口腔内部的空间，舌尖放松，便发出 /r/ 音了。忘记母语来练习发音，完全按照全新的口型去学习这些音标的发音，这很重要。

七、thin VS thing VS sing

- Uncle Bear is thin. 熊叔挺瘦的。
- I don't know a thing about this. 对此我一点儿都不了解。
- Uncle Bear can't sing very well. 熊叔唱歌唱得不太好。

这一组单词比较了两组发音，一组是 n 和 ng 两种不同的鼻音的发音，另一组是 s 和 th 两种不同的辅音的发音。其中 s 和 th 前面已经做过了比较，发音时口型区别比较大，这里我们重点比较两个鼻音的发音。当我们发 /n/ 时，舌尖上翘到上齿龈处，鼻腔施加压力。当我们发 ng 的"大鼻音"时，需要我们把舌尖放下，舌头的中后部抬起来，顶住上颚的后方，然后鼻腔发声。ng 的"大鼻音"发起来比较靠后，也会比较"累"。

八、lack VS like

- Your lack of experience is not the reason.
  你缺乏经验并不是理由。
- You like Uncle Bear? 你喜欢熊叔吗？

这一组单词主要比较的是 /æ/ 和 /aɪ/ 的发音。其实当我们系统地学过音标后，这两个音就非常容易区分了，前者是单元音，只有一个口型；后者是双元音，是由两个口型自然地过渡而产生的。如果你觉得两者的发音听上去很像，基本只有一个原因，就是你的双元音没有发出"双"的感觉来。/æ/ 和 /aɪ/ 发音的起点非常接近，如果你发 /aɪ/ 音时只发个开头的部分，那听上去和 /æ/ 便会比较像。双元音是我们以汉语为母语的英语学习者发音时的一大障碍，一定要仔细寻找那种给自己的嘴巴做瑜伽的感觉，掌握每个双元音的起点口型和落点口型，把每个双元音都发到位。

九、word VS world

- I need a word with you. 我需要跟你聊一聊。
- You are my world. 你是我的全世界。

这两个单词会给人一种发音差不多的错觉，单词 world 比 word 多了一个字母 l，大家之所以会觉得二者发音差不多，是因为 /l/ 音没有发到位。我们把这两个单词后面的字母 d 去掉，对比发 "wor" 和 "worl" 的音，后者结尾明显要把舌尖舔到上齿龈发 /l/ 的音。然后我们再把字母 d 补回来，这样 word 和 world 的发音就可以轻松区分开了。练习发音时，一定要放慢语速。

十、cycle VS psycho

- the cycle of life 生命的轮回
- He was a total psycho! 他是个十足的神经病！

这两个单词主要比较的是组成音节 /kl/ 和 /ko/ 的发音区别。单词中，当爆破音遇到 l 音，如 cycle 的 cle、little 的 tle、dribble 的 ble 等，都会组成一个单独的音节。在有些词典中，会将音标标记成 /kl/、/tl/、/bl/ 等，有些词典中会多加一个 /ə/ 音，形成 /kəl/、/təl/、/bəl/ 等，但是发音是一样的。爆破音 +/l/ 的发音要点，仍然是音节后面的舌尖舔到上齿龈处，这样 cycle 发完了之后，舌尖是在上齿龈的位置。而 psycho 则是以 /əʊ/ 或美音音标 /o/ 结尾，舌尖平放在口腔中。这样的话，cycle 和 psycho 虽然听上去很像，但是我们通过口型就可以轻松将二者区分开了。

十一、corporation VS cooperation

- He works for a large corporation. 他在一家大公司工作。
- Thank you for your cooperation. 感谢您的合作。

熊叔之前出席了某公司的一场大型庆典，女主持人将"Thank you for your cooperation"说成了"Thank you for your corporation"，翻译过来就是"感谢大家的公司"。对于在场不懂汉语的外国人来说，这便很困惑。

Cooperation 在发音时，音节要划分好，co-o-pe-ra-tion，很多人会犯的错误就是把前面的 co-o 发成一个 or 的音。需要知道的是，co 是非重读音节，o 是次重读音节，所以 co-o 连在一起发音的时候，要把 o 音读得相对更重一些，所以无论如何，co-o 和 cor 的发音区别还是很大的，前者是两个音节，后者是一个音节，而且后者在美音发音中还会有卷舌音。

十二、fight VS height

- I'm not going to fight you. 我不会打你的。
- My dog is afraid of heights. 我家的狗恐高。

对于沙县小吃，大家应该都比较熟悉。关于沙县小吃，流传着这样一个故事。

有一个人开着车去沙县小吃吃饭，因为时间比较赶，所以便直接把车停到了饭店门口，问老板："老板，我把车停在这里会不会被罚？"老板回答说："不会罚，不会罚。"

结果这个人吃完饭后到门口一看，车上有一张罚单，赶紧去找老板，气愤地说："老板，你不是说不会被罚吗！"

老板查看以后说："哪里罚（划）了，没看见呢，没被罚（划）啊！"

在中国，由于方言的原因有部分地区的人会分不清"罚"和"划"的发音，这便导致了某些同学在学英语的时候，也会分不清 f 和 h 的发音。因此，我们在学英语发音的时候，尽量不要受到母语发音的影响，哪怕某些音听上去和汉语很像，也不要被套进去，只有学好每个音发音时的口型，才能真正区分开这些易混淆的音。

在英语中，/f/ 是唇齿摩擦音，由上齿摩擦下唇，气流通过产生的；而 /h/ 的发音是"嗓子眼儿里的一口气"，和 /f/ 的发音差很远，区分起来应该很简单。

十三、honey VS horny

之前听说了这样一个故事：一位年轻的女子去国外旅游，在酒店吃早饭时想吃蜂蜜，就对服务员说："Honey?Honey?"但是由于发音非常不标准，导致服务员听到的是"Horny? Horny?"大家可以自行查找一下 horny 这个词的意思，比较不和谐，所以当时情境下服务员的表情非常尴尬。

在美式英语中，horny 是有卷舌音的，和 honey 的发音有很明显的区别。在国外的时候，如果想喝蜂蜜一定要想好了"honey"的发音再开口，不要闹出笑话。

十四、house VS horse

- I have a big house. 我有一个大房子。
- I have a big horse. 我有一匹高大的马。

house 是个双元音，起点口型较大，往 /ʊ/ 的口型上滑动，嘴巴在空中画了一个圈。而 horse 是个卷舌音，嘴巴口型不大，呈圆形，且要卷舌，这样便可以轻松区分开这两个单词的发音。

简单总结一下：很多易混淆的发音，都是因为大家在练习的过程中，只对听到的声音进行辨别，而不是去对这些发音的口型进行辨别。很多同学在学基础发音时，就是对听到的声音进行模仿。但是有些音在发音上听上去很像，甚至会和汉语中的某些发音相近，如果你不了解这些音在发音时口型的特点，那么很容易将音发错，时间长了，想改正就很难了。

所以我们要清楚地了解每个音标发音时的口型，不要受母语的影响，要认真、完整地去学习每个音标发音时的口型，再去开口练习。记住一句话：能读出来的，就一定能听懂。只要你能把每个音都发标准，那么你听到这些音时，就不会再有问题了。

3
CHAPTER

连读的发音技巧

cheese　　cheese

英语中的连读是什么样的呢？

首先我们要明白连读现象是如何产生的。前面熊叔提到，英语这种语言的节奏像流水一般，音与音之间会"自然地滑过"。那么为了保证两个单词之间的音能够"自然地滑过"，不间断，从而便产生了连读现象。

关注微信公众号"熊叔英语"，回复"我爱英语连读"，收听本章内容的音频讲解以及跟读训练。

◎ 连读现象一：辅音＋元音

这是最简单的连读类型。辅音＋元音是指前一个单词的结尾是辅音，后一个单词的开头是元音。这个时候我们把前面单词最后的辅音和后面单词开头的元音连起来读就可以了。连读的时候听上去就像一个单词。

我们先来看合成词的例子：

handover   makeup

grown-up

　　这些词的音标会有很明显的音节划分。比如，handover ['hændəʊvə]（美式音标 ['hændovɚ]），其中有很明显的音节划分 han-do-ver，我们在读的时候会很自然地把 d 和 o 进行连读。makeup 也是同理，读作"ma-kup"。grown-up，读作"grow-nup"。

　　词内连读读起来比较容易，而词与词之间的连读，其实也并不难。比如：

an apple　　　　　　　　an orange

按照上面的规律，我们读作：

a-na-pple　　　　　　　a-no-range

　　虽然是两个单词，但是连读后听上去就像一个词。所以很多外国人会把"天安门"读成"tia-nan-men"。

　　我们来看看常用的句子中的连读情况：

My name is Uncle Bear.
I'm 52 years old.
I'm going to pick up a friend.

连读起来的感觉大致应该是：
My na-mei-sUn-cle Bear. 中间的 is 被分解了。

I'm 52 year-sold. "我今年 52 岁"。注意不要因为连读影响单词的重读。比如，这里的标注很可能会让你认为重读部分是"sold"这个部分，但是并不是这样，因为这句话里最重要的部分是"52"。

I'm going to pi-cku-pa-friend. 这句话和第一句一样，有些连读部分，需要一鼓作气读完。另外，这里需要连读的音都是短元音，所以在朗读的时候，可以非常有节奏感。

难点提炼：连读时，前面的辅音是鼻音、/l/ 音、唇齿摩擦音时连读起来会相对较难。比如：

singer   sing a song
spell it   Life of Pie

其中，singer 和 sing a song 都是"大鼻音"的连读，难度大的地方在于这个鼻音本身。当"大鼻音"还没完全发完整的时候，和下一个元音连起来组成新的音节，发音时会有种错觉，好像这个音节是从鼻子里发出来的一样。

spell it，是 /l/ 音的连读。我们都知道这个音在音节开头或者结尾的地方发音不一样。连读的时候，按照正常的口型，spell 发到 /l/ 的时候，不要发完整，然后 /l/ 和后面的 it 连起来，相当于发"lit"之前要做一个"spe"到"l"的口型上的过渡。

前几年流行一首歌 Black Beatles，其中一句歌词是：That girl is a real crowd pleaser. 大家可以感受一下这句话的连读。

Life of Pie 的连读是唇齿摩擦音和元音的连读，难度本身在于

唇齿摩擦音 /f/ 或者 /v/。只要时刻记得这两个音的发音方式，这个连读就可以做到标准、地道。

请大家大声朗读下面的句子。

1. I'm working on it.

2. Hold on, please.

3. We need to sell it.

4. Cuz (because) when our love seems to fade away…

5. I'm from MA, my number is 6070-8090.

如果大家对连读不是很熟练的话，建议大家在练习之前先做一些标注。还记得前面说过的标记法吗？这里可以开始用起来了。类似于这样的连读，熊叔喜欢用下划线连起相应的字母表示连读。

1. I'm working on it.

2. Hold on, please.

3. We need to sell it.

4. Cuz (because) when our love seems to fade away…

5. I'm from MA, my number is 6070-8090.

再来一组有难度的：

1. You are so full of it.
2. Pick it up.
3. Take it away.
4. I'm an American.

下面，尝试在没有任何标记的情况下朗读下面两个句子：

1. It's not always easy, but we're making it work.
2. We have set up a system.

对照下面熊叔的标记，你找出所有的连读了吗？

1. It's not always easy, but we're making it work.
2. We have set up a system.

◎ 连读现象二：/d/ 或 /t/+/j/

在英语的一般过去时态中，最常见的表示疑问的句型为：

Did you…

　　读这样的句子时，did you 便会连在一起读，即 /d/+/j/ 的连读现象。类似的句型还有很多。比如：

Would you like a cup of coffee?

Did you do it last week?

What did you do?

　　仔细听，你会发现，/d/+/j/ 会被读成了 /dʒ/ + /j/。结合第一种连读现象，上面三句话会读成（美式音标）：

- Would you like a cup of coffee?

　/wʊ dʒju laɪ kə kʌ pəv 'kɔfi/

- Did you do it last week?

　/dɪ dʒju du ɪt læst wik/

- What did you do?

　/hwɑt dɪ dʒju du/

　　当 /t/ 遇上 /j/ 的时候发音会发生怎样的变化？首先，我们需要搞清楚 /t/ 和 /d/ 的关系。/t/ 和 /d/ 是相同的口型，前者发音时声带不振动，后者发音时声带振动。

　　/d/+/j/ 变成了 /dʒ/ + /j/。

　　/t/ +/j/ 就会读成 /tʃ/+/j/。

　　比如：

I went there last year.

What about you?

Let you go.

三句话当中的画线连读部分，都会读成 /tʃ/。

还有一种特殊情况：当 /s/ 遇上 /j/。这个情况的特殊之处在于，我们完全可以按照音标本身的方式去连读，也可以把 /s/ 发成 /ʃ/ 音去连读。比如：

I miss you.

读成：/aɪ mɪ sju/

或者：/ aɪ mɪ ʃju/

如果你需要对连读进行标注，那么你可以这样：

lastʃ year

What didʒ you do?

直接把变化的音补上去。当熟练了之后，就可以像第一种连读那样直接用下划线连接即可。

来大声朗读下面的句子吧：

1. Where did you go for dinner yesterday?

2. Would you mind closing the window for me?

3. Your parents are thinking about you.

4. They never want to let you go.

5. I miss you so much!

◎ 连读现象三：爆破音 + 辅音

大家都知道，/t/、/d/、/k/、/g/、/p/、/b/ 等有气流爆破的音被称为爆破音。当前一个单词以爆破音结尾，后一个单词以辅音开头的时候，这个爆破音就不能正常爆破了。

还记得我们说过英语中词与词之间的发音要"自然地滑过"吗？当爆破音遇到其他辅音时，往往会因为口型的过渡，导致自身失去了"爆破"。

比如，a good student，我们中国人的习惯是把 good 的 d 音发得很重，甚至发成"gooda student"。其实我们在发 d 音的时候就要注意，这只是一个辅音，气流冲一下，声音瞬间就结束了，不要拖泥带水。当 good 的 d 遇到后面的 student 的时候，d 的发音在口型刚做出来的时候便要过渡到 student 的发音，d 音的气流就没有了。也就是说，在这种连读里，前面的爆破音只做口型，不出声音。慢动作回放一下就是：先发"goo"，然后口型做到 d 音，准备发出 d 的声音的一瞬间，转而马上发 student 的音。

这种情况的连读，我们先从读单词练起：handsome，treatment。

这两个单词中的前一个音节的 /d/ 和 /t/ 都会失去爆破。标注方式上，熊叔喜欢用 handsome, treatment 这样的方式来标记。

下面我们进入句子的练习：

I just didn't get the chance.

I'm a good student.

It's up to you.

I've heard so much about you.

我们再来看看之前练过的绕口令：

How much wood would a woodchuck chuck if a woodchuck

could chuck wood?

特殊情况：当前面的爆破音和后面的辅音相同时，如 went

to，这种情况下只发后面的 t，并且会将该音稍微拉长。

偷懒的方法：连读的时候，如果大家觉得发音时做口型比较

难，也可以直接把发这个音时的口型省略。当你的发音足够流利

时，没人能听出来你是否真的把口型做到位了。

辅音连缀 pl、pr、bl、br、cl、cr 等这类连在一起的辅音在朗

读时，一定不要在两个辅音之间添加元音。比如：

please   pray

glass   brunch

◎ 连读现象四：元音 + 元音

我们在学双元音的时候，提到过两个元音之间口型的"过渡"。如果能掌握这个"过渡"，我们在连读元音 + 元音时就不会存在问题。

我们来看下面的几个例子：

two apples   three apples

four apples

如果你把外国人或者熊叔读这几个词组时的语速放慢十倍，你会听出 two 和 apples 之间会有一个过渡。two 最后的口型是什么样的？放慢 two 的发音，保持这个单词最后的口型，然后你从这个口型过渡到 apples，如果要保证声音不产生间隙，那么一定会有一个过渡的 /w/ 音的口型出现。three apples 也是一样，放慢体会，three 的最后口型是什么样子？过渡到 apples 会怎么样？这期间会有一个过渡的 /j/ 音的口型出现。那么 four apples 呢？其中的过渡音，就是卷舌音 /r/ 了。不过也要注意，出现的 /w/、/j/、/r/ 等，都只是作为过渡的口型而已，并不是完整的发音，起到润滑口型的作用。

这种连读，其实在单词内部就出现过。比如，liaison、cooperation、rearrange 等。我们在发这些单词的音的时候会感到困难，或者总觉得发得不顺畅，就是因为单词的发音涉及了元音之间的连读。

liaison（美式音标 /lɪˈezɑn/）中 i 和 ai 之间，明显是需要一个过渡口型的。

cooperation（美式音标 /koˌɑpəˈreʃən/），很多人会读成 corporation（美式音标 /ˌkɔrpəˈreʃən/）。"co-opera" 中间有很明显的重音变化，而且 co 和 op 之间也会有过渡口型的出现。

rearrange（美式音标 /ˌriəˈrendʒ/）中 re-a 在这里简直就像双元音一样地存在。

我们再来看看下面几个句子：

Go away.

I also need the other one.

I'd go anywhere for you.

Let me take care of you.

这里再次强调，过渡音不要发得过分，仅仅起到过渡作用就可以了。这两个句子往往会读作（熊叔喜欢用字体较小的 w、y、r 来标注这样的连读）：

Go w away.

I y also need the y other one. 注意介词 the 遇到后面开头是元音的单词或者起强调作用时，发音会变成 /ði/。

I'd go w anywhere for you.

Let me take care r of you.

元音和元音的连读在 there be 句型当中很常见，我们再来练习几个句子：

There are two apples.

There is an hour.

I asked you a question.

简单标注一下：

There r are two w apples.

There r is an hour.

I j asked you w a question.

第三句话中，不要忘记 asked 的 ed 发 /t/ 的音，和后面的 you 会有连读现象。

下面，我们通过一段对话来进行以上四种连读的综合训练：

Uncle Bear went to lunch in a small restaurant.

Uncle Bear: Hey, waiter. Can you come here for a second?

Waiter: Is there something wrong?

Uncle Bear: There is a hair in the salad. I mean, look at me. We both know it's not my hair.

Waiter: Oh, I'm so sorry. I'll go and get a new one for you.

Uncle Bear: And also, this soup is cold.

Waiter: I'm really sorry. I'll bring you a hot one right away.

…

Waiter: Sir, the manager said you don't have to pay for the meal. We're really sorry for what happened.

But Uncle Bear doesn't have any hair... Where did the hair come from?

下面是参考标注版本（你还能找出其他未标注的连读现象吗？）：

Uncle Bear went to lunch in a small restaurant.

Uncle Bear: Hey, waiter. Can you come here for r a second?

Waiter: Is there something wrong?

Uncle Bear: There r is a hair r in the salad. I mean, look at me. We both know it's not my hair.

Waiter: Oh, I'm so sorry. I'll go and get a new one for you.

Uncle Bear: And also, this soup is cold.

Waiter: I'm really sorry. I'll bring you a hot one right away.

…

Waiter: Sir, the manager said you don't have to pay for the meal. We're really sorry for what happened.

But Uncle Bear doesn't have any hair... Where did the hair come from?

4

CHAPTER

句子中的
重读和弱读

如果你的音标发音足够标准，那么你只要把上一章中的几种连读现象练好，你的发音就可以得到很大的改善。当然，这还不够，这只是我们在学习英语发音的过程中比较基础的发音技巧。我们还要学习的发音技巧包括：弱读、重读、缩读、语调训练、非重读音节中的 t 等，我们还要对句子的节奏进行训练。

关注微信公众号"熊叔英语"，回复"高阶发音技巧"，收听本章内容的音频讲解以及跟读训练。

我们首先来了解一下单词的重读。

我们在查字典的时候，往往会看到多音节单词的音标中有"'"或者"ˌ"符号的出现。比如 responsibility，美式音标为 [rɪˌspɑːnsə'bɪləti]。其中的"'"和"ˌ"分别代表重读和次重读，通俗来讲，就是"'"所在的音节读得最重，"ˌ"所在的音节读得次重。那如果以书写的大小来反映音节的重读程度的话，大概是这样：

其实我们汉语里也是有重读的。比如，"家伙"这个词，大家会读成：

家伙

不会读成：

家伙

在美式英语中，有些单词的重音可能和大家一直以来的印象不太一样。比如：February, necessary。它们的美式音标分别是：/ˈfɛbruˌɛri/, /ˈnɛsəˌsɛri/。

我们会看到，次重读音节处于倒数第二个音节，所以读起来是：

February　　　　　　　necessary

当多个单词组成表达甚至句子时，重读和弱读的节奏便更加明显。

一个词组成的句子也会有重读的部分：

(No!) No-oo!　　　　(God!) Go-od!

把一个单词拖长，前半部分重读，后半部分弱读，但仍然是一个单词。

来看一些两个词的表达：

call him 中明显 call 要重读

right now 中两个词读音的轻重程度差不多

go shopping 中第二个词读音更重一些

来看一些三个词的表达：

pick me up   take me down
up to you   take it easy

同一句话中，重音的位置不同，所表达的效果也会有所不同。比如：

I like you.（喜欢，不是爱，或者强调"喜欢"）

I like you.（我喜欢你，不是熊叔，或者强调"你"）

I teach English.（我教英语，不是教法语或西班牙语。）

I teach English.（所以不需要再给我推销英语培训课程了。）

This is wrong.（这件事错了，强调"这件事"，不是别的事。）
This is wrong.（强调这件事"错了"这个事实。）

在句子当中，重音的节奏会更加明显。句子中总有些词会重读，有些词会弱读。那么，怎样来区分重读和弱读呢？

重读有两种方式：逻辑重读和实词重读。

逻辑重读：重读一句话中相对来说含义比较重要的单词。

实词重读：重读句子中的实词。所谓实词就是有实际意义的词，如名词、动词、形容词、副词等，与之相对的是虚词，也是以功能性为主的词，如冠词、连词等。当然特殊情况除外。

熊叔的建议是：将两者结合起来练习。

比如，我们来看下面的一句话：

Uncle Bear bought a black bike at the store last night.
按照实词重读的规律，重读起来是这样的：

Uncle Bear bought a black bike at the store last night.
当你按照这样的方式去重读的时候，听上去会让人感到很不自然，所以这个时候我们要加上逻辑重音。看看这句话中，你最想强调什么信息？

Uncle Bear bought a black bike at the store last night.
（是熊叔买的，不是熊婶或熊小妹。）

Uncle Bear *bought* a black bike at the store last night.
（是熊叔买的，不是熊叔借的或者卖的。）

Uncle Bear bought a *black* bike at the store last night.
（熊叔买的是黑色自行车，不是其他颜色。）

Uncle Bear bought a black *bike* at the store last night.
（熊叔买的是自行车，不是汽车或马车。）

Uncle Bear bought a black bike at the *store* last night.
（熊叔在那家商店里买的自行车，不是在网上或者其他地方。）

Uncle Bear bought a black bike at the store *last night*.
（熊叔是昨天晚上买的，不是上周或者上个月。）

当然，在一句话当中，你也可以同时强调多个信息，使之有多处重读。即便如此，你会发现，类似于 at、the 等功能性的虚词在句子当中是很少会被重读的。

我们再来看下面的两个句子。大家想想，如果要得到熊叔所说的效果，应该怎么去读？

1. Uncle Bear is not married.
   强调"熊叔"没结婚，不是别人，是熊叔。
   强调他"没"结婚，是大龄"待嫁"男青年。

2. She just told me that she got engaged yesterday.
   强调是"她"告诉我的，不是别人告诉我的。

强调她"刚刚"告诉我，以及"订婚了"。

强调她"昨天"订婚这个时间点。

很明显，我们应该分别读成：

1. Uncle Bear is not married.

强调"熊叔"没结婚，不是别人，是熊叔。

Uncle Bear is not married.

强调他"没"结婚，大龄"待嫁"男青年。

2. She just told me that she got engaged yesterday.

强调"她"告诉我的，不是别人告诉我的。

She just told me that she got engaged yesterday.

强调她"刚刚"告诉我，以及"订婚了"。

She just told me that she got engaged yesterday.

强调她"昨天"订婚这个时间点。

在句子里，有重读就会有弱读。很多弱读比较简单，读轻一点儿就可以了，但是有些单词的弱读会发生发音的改变。

先看单个单词的弱读：

第一类，弱读成 /ə/ 或 /ɚ/ 的音，例如：

to — /tə/　　　　　from — /frəm/

at — /ət/　　　　　that — /ðət/

what —/wət/　　　　and — /ənd/

have — /həv/（助动词时）　　can — /kən/

am — /əm/　　　　for — /fə/

you — /jə/　　　　do — /də/（助动词时）

　　要注意区分这些词的使用场景，当这些词作为功能性词时，一般可以弱读，但是有实际意义时要想清楚是否可以弱读。

　　比如，Do you know that he's gay? 这里的 do 就可以弱读。

　　但是，当举办婚礼的时候，通常会有如下问答：

　　— Do you take this man to be your husband?

　　— Yes, I do.

　　这里的回答"Yes, I do."中的 do 往往不能弱读，而是需要重读的。

　　接下来，我们来看看句子中的弱读：

　　1. I'm *from* China. 读成 I'm /frəm/ China.

　　2. I said *that* I needed *to* leave. 读成 I said /ðət/ I needed /tə/ leave.

　　3. *And* now, please welcome Uncle Bear! 读成 /ən/ now, please welcome Uncle Bear.

第二类，弱读失去元音、辅音类，例如：

to — /t/，可以在句子中标注成 t'

do — /d/（助动词时）

but — /bt/，可以在句子中标注成 b't

and — /n/，可以在句子中标注成 'n

some — /sm/，可以在句子中标注成 s'm

come — /km/，可以在句子中标注成 c'm

have — /hv/（助动词时），可以在句子中标注成 h'v

must — /ms/，可以在句子中标注成 m'st

the — /ð/，可以在句子中标注成 th'

them — /əm/，可以在句子中标注成 'em

could — /kd/　　　　would — /wd/

believe — b'lieve　　today — t'day

tomorrow — t'morrow　　something — s'm'n

我们看看在句子中的体现：

1. *Come* on! 读成 /km/ on！

2. *Could you* lend me *some* money? 读成 /kd/ /jə/ lend me /sm/ money?

3. *But* that's not *the* case. 读成 /b/ that's not /ð/ case!（也可以选择弱读 that。）

第三类，音节变化类，例如：

because — /kəz/   going to — gonna

want to — wanna   have/have got — got

have got to — gotta   give me — gimme

我们同样来看几个句子：

1. *Because* you're wrong. 读成 /kəz/ you're wrong.

2. I'm *going to* have dinner with her. 读成 I'm gonna have dinner with her.

3. I *have got to* go. 读成 I gotta go.

4. I *want to* talk *to* you about *something*. 读成 I wanna talk t' you about s'm'n.

特殊的弱读：

can、can't，两个单词的音标分别是 /kæn/ 和 /kænt/。

但是我们知道，当 can't 后面接其他辅音时，结尾的 t 是会失去爆破的，这个时候和 can 就很难区分了，该怎么办呢？

当我们正常说一个含有 can 的句子时，一般来讲，当你不去特别强调"can"这个词的时候，can 会和第一类单词一样弱读读成 /kən/。比如：

I can do it!

I can speak English, French and Spanish.

会读成：

I /kən/*do* it!

I /kən/speak *English*, *French* and *Spanish*.

can 在句子中读音非常弱，一嘴带过。而在句子中需要强调"can"的时候，则会重读成 /kæn/。比如，奥巴马当年竞选总统时著名的演讲词：

Yes we can! To *Justice* and *Equality*!

Yes we can! To *Opportunity* and *Prosperity*!

会读成：

Yes we /kæn/! To Justice and Equality!

Yes we /kæn/! To Opportunity and Prosperity!

can't 在句子当中，不管是否被强调都会正常按照音标发音并且失去爆破。

听听下面的句子，熊叔读的是"能"还是"不能"？

1. I _____ do this!

2. I _____ afford a house like that!

下面我们来实战演练一下，这里选择的素材是实战利器《老友记》中第六季第二集中的一段对话。

不区分连读、重读、弱读

Joey: Oh my God! You're pregnant!

Chandler: No-o-o! (To Monica) No? (She nods no.) No-o-o! Look Joey, here's the thing, Monica and I have decided to live together, here. So, I'm gonna be moving out man.

Joey: Wow! (Tearing up) Well, uh… Hey! I'm really happy for you guys! Congratulations! (Kisses Monica on the cheek) See you later. (Starts for the door on the verge of tears as Monica stops him.)

Monica: Wait! Joey! Joey! Are you okay?!

Joey: Yeah, I gotta go! I got an acting job. (Turns towards the door, pauses, and turns back.) Like you'd believe that. This sucks!

Chandler: Look, I-I'm just gonna be right across the hall and I promise you, the minute Monica and I break up I'm moving right back in with you!

Joey: (To Monica) Okay! Look-look-look, uh, if you're gonna be moving in with him I feel it's my responsibility to tell you the truth about him! Okay? He's a terrible roommate! Terrible! He uh, forgets to umm… Oh-oh he always, he always umm—Oh, who am I kidding! He's the best roommate ever! (Hugs Chandler.)

区分连读、重读、弱读

Joey: Oh my **God**! You're **pregnant**!

Chandler: No-o-o! (To Monica) No? (She nods no.) **No**-o-o! Look **Joey**, **here's** the **thing**, **Monica** and I h'v decided to **live** together, **here**. So, I'm gonna be **moving out** man.

Joey: Wow! (Tearing up) Well, uh… **Hey**! I'm **really happy** for you guys! **Congratulations**! (Kisses Monica on the cheek) See you later. (Starts for the door on the verge of tears as Monica stops him.)

Monica: Wa-it! Joey! Joey! Are you **okay**?!

Joey: Yeah, I gotta go! I got an **acting** job. (Turns towards the door, pauses, and turns back.) Like you'd believe **that**. This **sucks**!

Chandler: Look, I-I'm just gonna be **right** across the hall and I **promise** you, the **minute** Monica　　and I **break up** I'm moving **right back in** with you!

Joey: (To Monica) Okay! Look-look-look, uh, if you're gonna be moving in with **him** I feel it's my **responsibility** to tell you the **truth** about **him**! Okay? He's a **terrible** roommate! **Terrible**! He uh, forgets to umm… Oh-oh he **always**, he always umm— Oh, who am I **kidding**! He's the **best** roommate ever! (Hugs Chandler.)

除了常见的连读、重读、弱读之外，我们会发现，going to 都读作 gonna，have got to 也都读成了 gotta。当然跟读美剧中的台词还是有难度的，所以如果想挑战《老友记》这种难度的素材，还是首先跟着熊叔做慢速的跟读训练吧！

5

高阶美式
发音技巧

本章的发音技巧讲解，聚焦美式发音特色，从歌词入手，练习地道的美语发音！

关注微信公众号"熊叔英语"，回复"地道美语技巧"，收听本章内容的音频讲解以及跟读训练。

◎ 美音中 /h/ 音的省略

讲 /h/ 音之前，先请大家听一段音乐。这首歌叫 *Havana*，演唱者是 Camila Cabello。其中有一段歌词是：

Oooh-oooh-ooh, I knew it when I met him
I loved him when I left him
Got me feelin' like
Oooh-oooh-ooh, and then I had to tell him
I had to go, oh na-na-na-na-na

Havana, ooh na-na (ayy)
Half of my heart is in Havana, ooh-na-na (ayy, ayy)
He took me back to East Atlanta, na-na-na (uh huh)
All of my heart is in Havana (ayy)

My heart is in Havana

Havana, ooh na-na

　　如果你仔细听，你会发现 met him、loved him、left him、tell him 等这些地方的 h 的发音都是听不到的，变成了"met im""loved im""left im""tell im"，h 前面的辅音直接和 h 后面的元音连读了，h 的发音便省略了。

　　其实消失的原因很容易理解，因为字母 h 发的 /h/ 这个音太弱了，弱到就只是一口气，所以被前面的强力辅音覆盖了，直接和后面的元音连读。第二段中 Havana 虽然也是 /h/ 开头，但是因为 Havana 是句子中要重点表达的单词，所以它不能和前面的词连读，/h/ 音就保留了下来。

　　所以，这段歌词会读成：

Oooh-oooh-ooh, I knew it when I met him

I loved h ed him when I left him

Got me feelin' like

Oooh-oooh-ooh, and then I had to tell him

I had to go, oh na-na-na-na-na

Havana, ooh na-na (ayy)

Half of my heart is in Havana, ooh-na-na (ayy, ayy)

He took me back to East Atlanta, na-na-na (uh huh)

All of my heart is in Havana (ayy)

My heart is in Havana

Havana, ooh na-na

不知道你有没有发现这两句话中有一个非常有意思的地方：

Half of my heart is in Havana, ooh-na-na (ayy, ayy)

He took me back to East Atlanta, na-na-na (uh huh)

Havana 后面吟唱的是 ohh-na-na。

那么按理说，East Atlanta 后面应该是 ta-ta-ta，但仍然是 na-na-na，这是为什么？我们将会在下一节中找到答案。

◎ 美音中 /nt/ 音的省略

大家尝试一下发 /n/ 和 /t/ 的音，如果前面的音标你已经学得很扎实的话，你应该能够感觉到，这两个音发音时的口型非常接近，只不过 /n/ 多了个鼻音。所以当你读 Atlanta 的时候，如果你读得很流利，就会读成 Atlanna。这便解释了为什么 East Atlanta 后面吟唱的不是 ta-ta-ta 而是 na-na-na 了。

同理，我们也就知道了为什么 want to 会弱读成 wanna，而不是 wantta。n 和 t 在一起的时候，/t/ 是干不过 /n/ 的。同样的，

don't have 或者 didn't have 也会读成 "don' 'ave" 和 "didn' 'ave"。

我们来练习下面几个句子：

- I don't understand. 我不理解。
- I want to go home. 我想回家。
- You can count on me. 你可以依靠我。
- Don't take it for granted. 不要想当然。
- I have a secret identity. 我有一个神秘的身份。

这些句子的连读：

- I don' understand.
- I wanna go home.
- You can coun on me.
- Don't take it for granned.
- I have a secret idennity.

有些时候，这个规律在连读中也适用。比如，isn't it 我们会读成 isn' it 的连读，n 的发音把 t 的发音覆盖了。再如，Isn't he? 这里的 n 的发音将 t 的发音覆盖了，同时后面的 h 的发音被省略了，于是 n 便与 e 发生了连读。

◎ 美音中 /t/ 音的"浊化"（其实并非浊化！）

有些同学认为美音中的 water 是读作"wader"的，甚至很多教发音的老师也会这样教学生。其实这是不标准的发音。

那么，这里的 /t/ 音到底有没有发生浊化呢？

如果用专业的术语来解释，这个发音现象是这样的：

当 /t/ 在非重读音节中的元音前时，且前一个音节以元音结尾时，会被读成不送气（失去爆破）的 /t/。

同时，这里需要注意的几点是：

1. 非重读音节是什么？

2. 如何发不送气的 /t/ 音？

首先可以肯定的是，/t/ 绝对没有完全浊化成 /d/。

非重读音节的关键词不必重读，也就是说，该音节一定不能是重读的音节。比如，attack 这个单词就不会有这样的发音现象。这个规律简单总结一下是：

第一，音节不重读；

第二，/t/ 所在的音节不能是单词的第一个音节；

第三，/t/ 前后被元音包围。

那么 today、tomorrow 这样的单词符合发音规律吗？答案是不符合。/t/ 所在的音节都是 to，虽然音节不重读，但是它们都在单词的第一个音节中。

那么，atom、letter 这样的单词符合发音规律吗？答案是符合。都是非重读的音节，/t/ 前后都是元音。

而 enter、Walter 符合规律吗？答案是不符合。虽然"ter"这个音节没有重读，但是 /t/ 前面的音标是辅音。

搞清楚规律之后，我们来看什么是"不送气的 /t/"。如果你学过法语或者西班牙语，应该会知道"不送气"的音是比较难发的。我们伸出手，放在嘴巴面前，放肆地发 /t/，有可能会有很多唾沫星子喷到你的手上。但是如果我们来尝试这样的动作：

当你马上要发 /t/ 音的时候，努力把这口气憋在嘴里，让你的手连气流都感受不到。

可以想象一下自己摆好发 /t/ 音的口型而准备发音的时候，突然打了个嗝。强硬地把这口气憋住，不让它爆破出去，你会发出一个既与 /d/ 音相类似，又与 /l/ 音相类似的音，这就是"不送气的 /t/"音。

我们来尝试读下面这几个单词，做发音练习：water，letter，atom。

相对而言，英国人对 /t/ 的处理方式则大不一样。他们有时候会省略这个 /t/ 音。比如句子 Where's the letter in the word letter? 会被读成：Where's the le'er t in the word le'er?

而句子 Would you like a cup of tea? 会被读成：Would you like a cup of lllllttttea[1]?

那么在美式发音中为什么会有这种"不送气"的 /t/ 音出现呢？

---

[1]　把 t 发的很重很夸张。

以 water 为例，可以对比一下按照音标的拼读和用不送气的 /t/ 去读，放慢速度多练习几次，你会发现正常的拼读会多出一步来！

当我们发完"wa"的时候，如果要把 /t/ 完整地发出来，需要把舌头从"wa"的位置调整到发 /t/ 音时的口型，然后 /t/ 完整地爆破出来再与"er"连读会比较拖沓，因为 /t/ 的爆破音需要我们的舌尖离开上齿龈向下走。在整个过程中，我们的舌尖位置是：

从下①（"wa"）到上②（t）再向下移③（t 的爆破）再移到卷舌④（"er"）。

而当 /t/ 不需要完整地爆破出来，也就是"不送气"的时候，我们的舌尖只需要从"wa"的口型过渡到"er"的口型，中间舌尖点一下发 /t/ 音时的口型就可以了。这个时候，我们的舌尖位置是：

从下①（"wa"）到上②（t）直接到卷舌③（"er"）。

In a word, 美式发音中出现这样的现象，其实是把 /t/ 音弱化了。所以如果你把它浊化，反而是加强了这个音，是反其道而行之，必然不好听。

接下来，我们大声朗读下面的单词，感受下"不送气"的 /t/ 音。

letter   water

writer   ·   better

reporter

把单词放在句子中再来读一读：

- I sent you a letter last month. 我上个月寄了一封信给你。
- Could you bring me some water? 你可以给我带点水吗？
- He's a terrible writer. 他是一个糟糕的作者。
- You can do much better! 你可以做得更好！
- I wanted to be a reporter. 我曾经想成为一名记者。(wanted 要读成什么来着？"wanned"！符合我们刚学过的 /nt/ 的发音规律。)

另外，在句子中有连读的时候，这个发音技巧也同样适用。比如，You have to let it go.

句子中，let 和 it 会连在一起读，我们就可以把它当作一个单词，这个时候 let 的 t 也会发出不送气的 /t/ 音。类似的组合会经常出现。比如，let it、it is、what is/are，甚至在朗读 let him、let her 的时候，/h/ 音也会被覆盖，也会出现这样的现象。

我们来试着读下面几个句子：

- Only know you love her when you let her go. 当你让她远离你的时候你才知道你是爱她的。
- Get it out of me! 把这弄开！
- What is this about? 这是关于什么的？
- I'm going to write her a check. 我要给她写张支票。

- I had always been slender, but soft somehow, obviously not an athlete. 我一直很苗条，但不知为何身体却很柔软，显然不是一个运动员。

- Betty bought a bit of better butter. But she said, this butter's bitter. If I put it in my batter, it'll make my batter bitter. 贝蒂买了一些更好的黄油，但她说，这黄油是苦的。如果我把它放进面糊里，我的面糊就会变苦。

当你在连读 let her 和 write her 的时候，有没有想过它们和 letter、writer 在发音上有什么区别？

其实，在句子当中，这两组在读音上的差距真的很小，尤其是当你在很自然地对话的时候。但如果一定要指出它们的区别来，我们可以将语速放慢十倍，let her 和 write her 的"er"音要比 letter 和 writer 的"er"音稍微重一些。但是在句子中，两组的"er"音都是弱读的，所以大家无须太在意如此细微的区别。不过有一点要注意，当你在句子中想强调"her"的时候，一定要重读。

比如，Let **her** do it. 你想强调的是，别人做不了这事儿，得让"她"去做，那这个时候，连 /h/ 音都可以保留了，反倒是前面 let 的 /t/ 音可以省略。

Let her do it.

另外，当句子中的"to"被弱读时，也会被弱读成"不送气"的 /t/ 音。

比如，Does my skin look looser **to** you. 这里的 to 首先被弱读

成"tuh"或"t"，然后会进一步把 t 的爆破也省略，只剩下不送气时的口型。

◎ 其他情况下失去爆破的发音

英语中，当 /t/、/p/、/k/ 出现在 /s/ 后面时，也会读成"不送气"的 /t/、/p/、/k/。比如：

student	school
speak	astonish

或许你会认为这里的 /t/、/p/、/k/ 发生了浊化，其实它们并没有完全浊化，只是失去了爆破，读成了"不送气"的版本。如果你觉得失去爆破的发音难度很大，熊叔教你一个简单的方法：把这三个音浊化后，读得弱一些就可以了。

我们来读一读下面几个句子：

- I'm not a student anymore. 我不再是一个学生了。
- I want to go back to school. 我想重返校园。
- Who's speaking? 谁在讲话？
- What you did really astonishes me. 你的所作所为真是让我吃惊。

◎ 当 /t/ 音遇上 /n/ 音——"喉塞音"

我们都知道，当 /n/ 在 /t/ 前面的时候，/n/ 的发音一般会重于 /t/ 的发音，那么如果反过来会是什么样的情况呢？当 /t/ 出现在 /n/ 之前，/t/ 的发音是否重于 /n/ 的发音？比如：certainly，mountain。

这两个单词中的 /t/ 都出现在 /n/ 的前面，这种发音现象我们可以将它称为"喉塞音"。"喉塞音"，通俗地理解就是 /t/ 音卡在喉咙处没有发出来。所以这两个词听上去很像是："cer'ainly"，"moun'ain"。

音标 /t/ 在发音时只做个口型，没有发出声音来。

我们来读一读下面几个句子：

— Could you do me a favor? 你可以帮我一个忙吗？

— Certainly! 当然可以！

Let's go hiking in the mountains this weekend! 我们这周末去徒步登山吧！

◎ 美音中的"卷舌音"

和英式发音相比，美式发音中最大的特色应该就是"卷舌音"了。我们在学音标的过程中基本已经学会了如何发"卷舌音"，也就是 /r/ 的发音。虽然叫"卷舌音"，但实际上我们的舌尖多数情况下只是向上翘，而没有真的"卷"到嘴里。在我们学过的音标当中，只要参考美式音标，就能明确哪些音该"卷"舌。

　　在这里重新提及卷舌音的目的是要提醒大家，在美式发音当中，有不少单词会让人情不自禁地卷舌，但实际上却不应该卷舌。比如：

famous　　　　　　　　breakfast

vicious　　　　　　　　wall

call

　　熊叔见过很多人会把这些词发成卷舌音。虽然发成卷舌音对方也能听懂你想表达的内容，但是你的口语发音听起来会很不标准。

　　famous、breakfast、vicious 这三个单词最后一个音节很容易被发成卷舌音，大家一定要注意！

　　wall、call 的结尾明明是 /l/ 音，也会有同学将它发成卷舌音，大家一定要注意！

　　卷舌音的标志是字母 r，没有 r 出现的地方一定不要乱发卷舌音！

　　请大家尝试慢速朗读下面的句子，注意哪些地方要发卷舌音，哪些地方不应该发卷舌音：

- Let's have breakfast together. 我们一起吃早餐吧。
- Uncle Bear is not famous. 熊叔不出名。
- Walls have ears. 隔墙有耳。
- Give me a call. 给我打个电话。

朗读下面的几个句子，需要发卷舌音的地方，熊叔已把对应的字母加粗：

- Let's have breakfast togeth**er**.
- Uncle Be**ar** is not famous.
- Walls have **ear**s.
- Give me a call.

◎ 番外篇 1：当美音中的 /æ/ 遇上 /r/

在美国中西部的口音当中，当 /æ/ 遇上 /r/ 的时候，有时 /æ/ 会读成 /ɛ/，如单词 Harry、embarrassing 等。

Harry 和 embarrassing 也就读成了：

Harry /ˈhɛri/

embarrassing /ɪmˈbɛrəsɪŋ/

当然，正常按照音标去读也是完全没有问题的。在这里，我们把这种变化当成美国的一种方言来介绍。

◎ 番外篇 2：美音当中的 "wh" 字母组合的发音

我们来看两个单词：whales 和 wales。whales 中的 "wh" 和 wales 中的 "w" 都发 /w/ 的音，似乎发音是一样的。

但是如果我们查阅标注为美式音标的词典时，就会发现 "wh" 这个字母组合的发音存在不一样的情况。

参考权威的 *Marriam Webster's Advanced Learners Dictionary*，"wh" 的音标是 /w/，但是如果参考《21 世纪词典》，会发现 "wh" 字母组合的美式音标为 /hw/。我们常见的 what、when、why 等，都存在这样的现象！

其实，不管 "wh" 组合是发 /hw/ 还是 /w/，我们可以将其理解为美国不同地区的口音。比如，纽约东北地区发 /hw/ 音的会多一些，所以我们在看美剧《老友记》时，Chandler 每次惊讶地发 "What！" 的时候，听上去的发音是 /hwɑt/。大家在练习发音的时候，"wh" 字母组合前面的 /h/ 可发可不发，影响不大。

下面在句子中感受一下两种发音风格的不同（音频中朗读第一遍时的发音为 /hw/，第二遍的发音为 /w/）：

- What are you doing? 你在做什么？
- Why are you doing this? 你为什么这么做？
- When did you do it? 你什么时候做的这件事？

6

CHAPTER

美音中各个
时态的发音技巧

在进行进一步的学习之前，我们先把学过的发音技巧结合起来做一个综合训练。我们在本章，会通过不同时态的句子来进行各个发音技巧的练习。在本章结束时你会发现，掌握了不同时态的发音特点，你几乎就能够掌握我们前面所学的所有发音技巧，并且能综合运用。我们从最简单的时态开始，练习最简单的发音技巧，再逐步进行深入练习，进而掌握复杂时态的复杂发音技巧。

英语语言的思维模式和汉语语言的思维模式有很大的不同，其中最明显的一点就体现在动词的使用上。英语中的动词，会有一个时间上的概念。举个简单的例子，"I loved you."看到这句话，我们第一反应可能会认为其含义就是"我爱你"。但是仔细想想，"I loved you"包含的意思并不只是"我爱你"那么简单。其实这句话包含了很多信息。Loved 这个动词不是原型，是过去式，也就代表了这个动作是过去发生的，所以这句话所包含的信息其实是"我在过去、在那时是爱你的"。

所以"I loved you"这句话更多的含义是：我爱过你。而且在发音上，这句话也不仅仅是字面上的拼读。按照我们前面所学的技巧，d 和 y 会连读发成 /dʒj/ 音。

再如，我去年买了块表，我打算明年再买块表。在汉语里表达不同时间段里的买东西的含义都用同一个汉字"买"，而在英语里，分别表述为"I bought a watch last year."和"I'm going to buy a watch next year."，表达不同时间段里的买东西的含义所用的英文单词是不一样的，所用动词存在词形上的变化。

　　英语中一共存在四个时四个态，加起来不同排列组合有 16 种时态，其中常用的时态有 10 种左右，可以参考下图（见下页），做绿色标识的为常用时态。不同的时态，在口头上也要配合不同的发音技巧才能读得标准，下面熊叔就给大家盘点一下不同时态需要的不同发音技巧。（本书聚焦发音，所以不会具体讲解某个时态的用法。）

　　关注微信公众号"熊叔英语"，回复"时态发音技巧"，收听本章内容的音频讲解以及跟读训练。

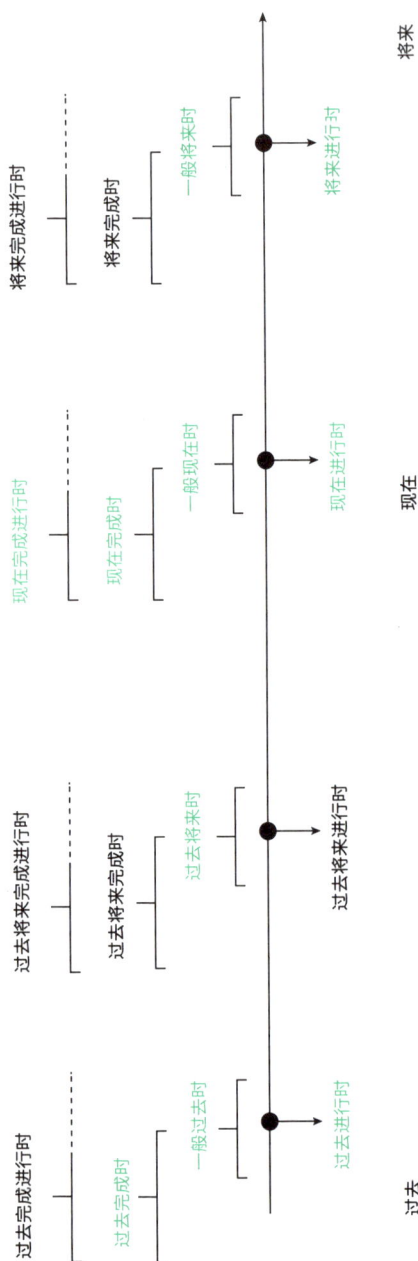

◎ 一般现在时的发音技巧

一般现在时是非常常见的时态。在这个时态当中，比较难发音的是动词的第三人称单数形式。

我们先来看看动词的第三人称单数形式的变化规则表（先有动词变化规律，后有动词第三人称单数形式的发音规律）：

大部分动词	+s	get – gets, drive - drives
以 /s/、/z/、/tʃ/、/ʃ/、/dʒ/、/ʒ/ 结尾的动词	+es	pass — passes, teach teaches, wash — washes
以辅音字母 +y 结尾的动词	y 变成 i, +es	study — studies
特殊情况	不规则	go — goes, do — does be — is, have — has

其中的发音规则是：

1. 大部分直接加 s 的动词，s 的发音取决于单词的最后一个音标，如果是清辅音，那么 s 发 /s/ 音；如果是浊辅音或者元音，那么 s 发 /z/ 音。

比如单词 get 的最后一个音标是 /t/，是清辅音，那么 get 的第三人称单数形式 gets 的发音就是 /gɛts/。

再如单词 drive 的最后一个音标是 /v/，是浊辅音，那么 drive 的第三人称单数形式 drives 的发音就是 / draɪvz/。

2. 加 es 的动词，es 的发音为 /ɪz/，如 teaches 的发音就是 /'titʃɪz/，

多了一个音节。

3. 以辅音字母 +y 结尾的动词变成第三人称单数形式后符合第一条发音规则。

4. 特殊情况要单独处理。其中，do 变成 does 后，元音发音也发生了变化，其发音为 /dʌz/。

当然，以上是官方的发音规则。你会发现，很多时候动词第三人称单数的结尾要发的 /z/ 音，实际在听的时候，似乎这个 /z/ 的音并不是很明显。没错！这个 /z/ 加到这里，其实已经处于整个单词读音最弱的地方了，所以没有人会刻意地把 /z/ 发得那么完整、那么到位。在句子当中，往往这个第三人称单数形式多出来的 /z/ 音，会被说话人一嘴带过，有时候听着和 /s/ 音差不多。下面，我们在句子中感受一下：

- He drives to work. 他开车上班。
- She goes shopping every weekend. 她每个周末都去购物。

但是，有连读情况的时候就要重视词末 s 的发音了。比如：

- He drives home. 他开车回家。
- He spends a lot of money. 他花了很多钱。

还有些句子，要搞清楚是哪些音发生了连读。比如：

- I get up early every day. 我每天都起得很早。
- She gets up late every day. 她每天都起得很晚。

这两句话当中，第一句的 get up 是"t"和 up 连读，而第二句中，gets up 是"ts"和 up 连读。

一般现在时的疑问句当中，经常会对第三者进行提问。比如：

- Does he have a lot of money? 他有很多钱吗？
- Does she know he has a lot of money? 她知道他有很多钱吗？

这里的 Does he 和 Does she 该怎么读呢？

Does 遇到 he 的时候，he 要弱读，h 的发音被覆盖，读成 Does he。

Does 遇到 she 的时候，does 结尾的 /z/ 音几乎听不到了，所以听上去很像是 Does she。

以上讲解的是含有一般现在时的句子的发音技巧。接下来，一起实战操练一下吧！我们来大声朗读下面的句子：

- Robin gets up at 7:15.（发音要点：gets 和 up 的连读）
- Then, she takes a shower at 7:30.（发音要点：takes 和 a 的连读）

- She gets dressed at 8:00.

- She has breakfast at 9:00.（发音要点：breakfast 注意后面不要有卷舌音）

- She brushes her teeth at 9:05.（发音要点：brushes 的尾音可以覆盖 her 的 /h/ 音）

- She goes to work at 9:10.

◎ 现在进行时的发音技巧

现在进行时一般以 be doing 的形式出现在句子当中。进行时发音的难点在于动词 +ing 之后，/ŋ/ 音很难发。你会发现很多外国人也懒得发这个音，所以在不少歌词里他们都会把 "ng" 的音简化成 "n'"。甚至日常打招呼的 How are you doing? 都被简化成了：How 'r y' doin'?

在现在进行时的句子当中，主要的发音难点有：动词 +ing 形式的连读、含有现在进行时的疑问句的读法、带有情绪的进行时态所在语句的读法。

1. 动词 +ing 形式的连读

我们来看下面几个句子：

- I'm making a cake. 我正在做蛋糕。
- I'm picking her up. 我来接她。
- He's doing his best. 他正尽最大努力做到最好。

在这三个句子当中，都存在 ing 和后面的单词发生连读的现象，分别是 ing+a、ing+her、ing+his，这就要求我们把"ng"的音发到位。我们来一起回顾一下这个音熊叔是怎样讲解的：

"熊叔把这个音称为'大鼻音'。发 /n/ 音时舌尖上翘，舔上齿龈，而发 /ŋ/ 音时舌身中部拱起，抵住上颚，舌身前部、舌尖自然下垂，声带振动，发出 /ŋ/ 音来。"

以单词 singer 为例我们分步来分析它的发音：

第一步发音为：发 si

第二步发音为：发 sing

第三步发音为：发 singer

鼻音是相对来说比较难发的音，"ng"的发音同样比较难发标准。所以在发鼻音的时候，大家可以先把鼻音的音标省略，然后再补上，进而把音发全。比如单词 down，你先发"dow"的音，然后再加上 n 的音，down 的发音就会更加标准。如果鼻音后面还有元音的话，往往会把鼻音拖长，使得鼻音前后的元音都会被这个鼻音所覆盖。举个简单的例子，句子中出现了 down on，那其实在连读之后，听上去更像是"down non"，而不是 down on。

那么，在读含有 ing+ 连读的现在进行时句子时，我们也可以分解来读。我们以 I'm making a cake 为例：

第一步发音为：发 I'm mak…

第二步发音为：发 I'm making…

第三步发音为：发 I'm making a… 听上去很像是 I'm making /ŋə/…

第四步发音为：发 I'm making a cake. 听上去很像是 I'm making /ŋə/ cake.

现在，我们再来重新朗读刚刚的那几句话：

- I'm making a cake.
- I'm picking her up.
- He's doing his best.

2. 含有现在进行时的疑问句的读法

疑问句分为一般疑问句和特殊疑问句。

含有现在进行时的一般疑问句的常见句型有：

Am I doing…?

Are you doing…?

Is he doing…?

Is she doing…?

Is it doing…?

Are we/they doing…?

含有现在进行时的特殊疑问句的常见句型有：

What am I doing…?

What are you doing…?

What is he doing…?

What is she doing…?

What are we/they doing…?

每个问句都有不同的发音技巧，我们一起来看一看。

- Am I doing…? 发音技巧：Am I 连读。

- Are you doing…? 发音技巧：把 you 弱读成 ya 或者 y。

- Is he doing…? 发音技巧：Is he 连读，/z/ 覆盖了 /h/。

- Is she doing…? 发音技巧：Is she 中的 /z/ 被覆盖。

- Is it doing…? 发音技巧：Is it 连读，注意 s 发的是 /z/，同时 it 的 /t/ 失去爆破，只做口型。

- Are we/they doing…? 发音技巧：弱读 we/they。不用刻意去改变 we/they 的发音，弱读即可。

- What am I doing…? 发音技巧：What am I 都连起来读，同时 what 的 /t/ 要读成不送气的 /t/。

- What are you doing…? 发音技巧：What are 连读，/t/ 同样不送气，并且 are 弱读成 /ə/。

- What is he doing…? 发音技巧：What is he 全部连读，/t/ 不送气，同时 is 的 /z/ 覆盖了 he 的 /h/。

- What is she doing…? 发音技巧：What is 连读，/t/ 不送气，同时 is 的 /z 省略。

• What are we/they doing...? 发音技巧：What 和 are 连读，/t/ 不送气，are 弱读成 /ə/，we/they 弱读。

这些发音技巧，我们在前面都已经讲过。所以你也可以把这里的发音训练当成综合性的技巧训练。

我们用下面的对话来做具体的练习：

Joey: Hey, Uncle Bear, **what are you doing here?**

Uncle: **What am I doing?** I came here to see you.

Joey: Oh really? Then **what is she doing here?**

Uncle: We came here together to apologize to you.

Joey: **Are you kidding?** Apologize for what?

Uncle: For... not paying you back.

Joey: **What are you talking about?** I don't remember lending you money!

Amy: What? Then **what are you fighting about?**

Joey: That's what he said! He said he didn't remember borrowing money from me!

Amy: Come on, you two. Grow up already! Uncle came to apologize! And he will pay you back!

Joey: Fine, Uncle. If you can get the money in a week, I guess we can still be friends.

3. 带有情绪的进行时态所在语句的读法

有些时候，我们还可以在现在进行时当中掺杂某种想要表达的情绪。比如，大家可以比较一下下面的两句话：

* He always asks me questions.
* He is always asking me questions.

第一句话偏向于描述事实，译为"他总是问我问题"，而第二句话里面则带有说话人的情绪了，这种情绪所要表达的含义可以是"他怎么那么多问题啊，好烦！"也可以是"你看这孩子多刻苦，总是有问题就去问老师！"

再如：

* He always helps others.
* He is always helping others.

从这两句话的对比中，我们可以看出第二句话中会带有说话者的情绪："这孩子真善良，总是助人为乐！"

产生这种情感现象的原因主要是：现在进行时，表示正在做某事，所以给人一种强烈的画面感。不仅是现在进行时，所有的进行时态，都会因此而产生一种"正在做某事"的画面感，从而可以产生出情绪来。在现在进行时的表达中加上"always"，情绪表现得就更明显了。

我们来大声朗读下面的句子：

- My daughter is always asking me for presents. 我的女儿总是问我要礼物。
- Uncle Bear is always making excuses for being late. 熊叔总是为他的迟到找借口。
- My relatives are always telling me that I should get good grades. 我的亲戚总是告诉我要取得好成绩。
- My parents are always trying to make me study more. 我的父母总是让我学得更多。

◎ 现在完成时的发音技巧

现在完成时主要由 have done 这个结构组成。这里的 have 也不再是有实际意义的动词，而是变成了助动词。所以对于现在完成时的句子来说，最适用的发音技巧就是 /h/ 音被覆盖，以及 have 的弱读。我们来分析下面几个句子包含了哪些发音技巧：

- What have you done? 你都做了什么？
- Has he finished the report? 他完成报告了吗？
- Has she done it yet? 她已经做完了吗？
- I have done it three times. 我已经做过三次了。

What have you done? 首先 /h/ 被 what 的 t 的发音覆盖，然后 have 弱读成 /əv/，what 也弱读成 /wət/，所以整个句子读起来，重音在 done 上，变成：

/wətəv/ you done?

第二句中的 Has，同样可以弱读成 /həz/，同时 /z/ 的音覆盖后面的 /h/，把句子重音放在后面 finished the report 上面。读成：

/hə'zi/ finished the report?

第三句中的 Has she，has 弱读后，/z/ 的音被省略，done it 连读，it 的 t 失去爆破，读成：

/ hə'ʃi/ done it yet?

你可能会想，it 和 yet 不也应该连读吗？在这里，由于 it 和 yet 的意思并不连贯，分别属于两个"意群"的内容，所以这里选择不连读。"意群"主要用于句子中的停顿和音节拖长。

最后一句中，I have 可以弱读成 I /həv/，后面的 done it 要连读。I have 更多适合直接缩写成 I've。

再来看几个句子，感受一下现在完成时的发音技巧：

- Have you told mom that you're not coming? 你告诉了妈妈你没来吗？

- Oh, I've done it so many times. 哦，我已经做过很多次了。

- She has been the best student so far. 她是迄今为止最好的学生。

- He has failed three exams this semester. 他这个学期已经挂科三次了。

◎ 现在完成进行时的发音技巧

现在完成进行时主要是以 have been doing 的结构出现在句子中的。have done 变成了 have been doing 之后，整个动词部分的朗读节奏发生了很大的变化。我们来看下面这个句子。

- I have been teaching English for more than ten years.

仔细听，你会发现，除了 have 常规弱读外，been 也弱读了。整个句子听上去就像：

- I h'v b'n teaching English for more than ten years.

have 和 been 都被弱读了。大部分时候，在现在完成进行时的句子中，我们都会弱读 have been，重读后面的动词。再来看下面几个句子：

- Uncle Bear! I've been waiting for you for two hours! 熊叔！我已经等你两个小时了！（发音要点：重音放在 you、waiting、 two hours 上）

• I have been working on that project for two months. Still it got me nowhere! 我已经在这个项目上耗费两个月了，但仍然没什么起色！（发音要点：重音放在 working、project、two months、nowhere 上）

• Uncle Bear has been writing this book for more than half a year now. 目前熊叔写这本书已经写了半年多了。(发音要点，has 弱读成 h's，been 常规弱读，重音放在 Uncle Bear、writing、book、half a year 上）

现在完成进行时还有一个特点，就是它拥有进行时态的画面感。这样的话，对于相同意思的两句话，现在完成进行时的表现力就更丰富了。比如下面的两句话：

• I have taught English for more than ten years.
• I have been teaching English for more than ten years.

第一句话所表达的是单纯的字面意思"熊叔已经教了十年英语了"；而第二句话会有动作进行的画面感，所表达的内容不仅仅是"熊叔已经教了十年英语了"。根据说话人不同的语气，第一句话可以包含多种情绪。比如，"熊叔已经教了十年英语了，头发都掉光了！""熊叔已经教了十年英语了，还在这儿凑字数卖书呢！"等。I have been teaching English，这句话会给人一种正在教书上课的画面感，从而让这句话蕴含了更多的情绪。那我们在使用现在完成进行时的时候，就可以在句子中加入自己的感情元素。

我们再来读几个句子：

- They've been dancing here for two hours, and they still don't want to leave. 他们已经在这里跳舞跳了两个小时了，还是不想离开。
- It's been raining for a week now. I miss the sun!
已经下了一周的雨了。我想念晴天！
- He has been doing the same thing over and over again for more than 40 years. 他已经重复做同一件事超过 40 年了。

你可以尝试在读这些句子的时候，加入一些个人的情绪在里面。

◎ 一般过去时的发音技巧

一般过去时的陈述句主要变化是动词变成了过去式。我们来看看动词变过去式的规律：

大部分动词	加 -ed，以字母 e 结尾直接加 -d	want — wanted live — lived
"辅音字母 +y" 结尾的动词	y 变成 i 再加 -ed	study — studied carry — carried
"元音字母 + 一个辅音字母" 结尾，且以重读音节结尾	双写末尾辅音字母再加 -ed	stop — stopped plan — planned
不规则动词	特殊变化	have — had，do — did， take — took，begin — began

　　我们看规则动词的变化，都是以 -ed 结尾。那么，结尾处 ed 的发音规律是怎样的呢？

ed 前是元音 / 浊辅音，发 /d/	ed 前是清辅音，发 /t/	ed 前是 /t/ 或 /d/，发 /ɪd/
carried	stopped	wanted
traveled	liked	started
learned	dropped	counted
loved	worked	busted

　　在这里需要额外指出的是，根据美音中 n 和 t 在一起的发音特点，wanted 又可以读作 /wɒnɪd/，发音过程中 /n/ 音覆盖了 /t/ 音。同样的，counted 读音中的 /n/ 音也可以覆盖 /t/ 音。

　　以上是这些动词变化后最基本的发音规则。当变形后的动词置于一句话当中时，需要练习的发音内容就更多了。

我们在讲连读时介绍了一个技巧，即当爆破音遇到其他辅音时，前面的爆破音要失去爆破。这个连读技巧在一般过去时所在的句子中非常常见，我们来看卜面两个句子：

- I liked the new boss.
- I loved the new boss.

这时候，liked 和 loved 的尾音 /t/ 和 /d/ 遇到了后面的 the，便失去爆破了。在发这个失去爆破的音时，只做口型，不出声音。

我们再来看看其他情况下 ed 的发音，比如下面几个句子：

- I loved you. 我爱你。
- I liked you. 我喜欢你。
- I stopped you. 我阻止了你。
- I wanted your book. 我想要你的书。
- I worked in an office before. 我之前在这间办公室工作。
- I carried a bag with me. 我带了个书包。

这些句子看似简单，但是却暗藏玄机。我们来依次分析一下。

I loved you，根据发音规则，loved 的结尾是 /d/ 音，那么 /d/ 音和 you 连读的时候应该怎么读呢？即 /d/ 发成了 /dʒ/。

然而，I liked you，根据发音规则，liked 中结尾的音是 /t/，/t/ 和 you 连读的发音情况还记得吗？即 /t/ 发成了 /tʃ/，所以 I loved you 和 I liked you 中的连读，是不一样的！

　　再来看句子 I stopped you 和 I wanted your book。根据上面的经验，应该能知道 stopped you 的连读中，ed 的 /t/ 发成了 /tʃ/，而 I wanted your book 中的 ed 发成了 /ɪd/，所以和 you 连读后读音就发成了 /ɪdʒ/。

　　再来看句子 I worked in an office before，这句话中的连读非常多，但是首先要清楚的是 worked 中的 ed 发的是 /t/ 音，所以和后面的 in 连读时，是 /t/ 在连读。同时根据美音中"不送气"的 /t/ 的发音现象，这里的 /t/ 又要发出 letter 中的"不送气"的 /t/。然后 in an office 也要连读，整个句子读起来就是：

I worked(/t/) in an office before.

　　最后 I carried a bag with me，也要搞清楚 carried 中的 ed 发的是 /d/ 音，然后和 a 连读，读成：

I carried/d/ a bag with me.

　　再来看看含有一般过去时的疑问句：

- What did you do?
- Did you do it last night?
- Did she do it last night?
- Did he do it last night?
- Did they do it last night?

相信讲到这里，大家应该已经能够自己识别句子中适用的发音技巧了。

- What did you do? 发音技巧：/t/ 失去爆破，did you 连读成 di/dʒ/ you。
- Did you do w it last night? 发音技巧：did you 连读成 di/dʒ/ you，do it 中间用 /w/ 的口型连接，/t/ 失去爆破。
- Did she do w it last night? 发音技巧：/d/ 和 /t/ 失去爆破，其他同上。
- Did he do w it last night? 发音技巧：/h/ 被 /d/ 覆盖，/d/ 直接和 /h/ 后的元音连读，其他同上。
- Did they do w it last night? 发音技巧：/d/ 失去爆破，其他同上。

最后来看看一般过去时中的情态动词。

常用的有单词 would、could、should 等，它们虽然是 will、can 和 shall 的过去式，但是也不仅仅用于过去式当中，很多时候这些词也用来表示一种委婉的说法。例如，should 本身也有"应该"的意思。此外，这些单词中的字母 l 都是不发音的。

在句子当中，它们有两种读法：重读时，读 /wʊd/、/kʊd/ 以及 /ʃʊd/。弱读时，读 /wəd/、/kəd/ 以及 /ʃəd/，甚至在个别情况下可以发成 /wd/、/kd/ 以及 /ʃd/。

当然也不要忘记，这些单词的尾音 /d/，连读元音、/j/ 或者失去爆破的情况大家都需要考虑到。请看下面几个句子：

- Could you do me a favor?（委婉说法，非过去式。）
- I should probably go. (should 表示应该，非过去式。)
- I would probably go there.（委婉说法，非过去式。）

下面，请大家运用连读技巧来朗读下面的句子：

- C'd you do me j a favor?
- I sh'd probably go.
- I w'd probably go there.

◎ 过去进行时、过去完成时、过去完成进行时的发音技巧

过去进行时一般的形式是：was/were doing，和现在进行时的发音技巧差不多。我们来看下面几个句子：

- I was having a lot of fun with my friends last night when you came.

- He was doing OK.
- We were talking about how Uncle Bear lost all his hair.

在练习过去进行时的句子时，除了要注意到动词 +ing 形式的发音规则外，也要把 was 和 were 进行弱读处理（除非要强调 was 或 were）。was 弱读成 w's，were 弱读成 /wə/。

- I w's having a lot of fun with my friends last night when you came.
- He w's doing OK.
- We /wə/ talking about / how w Uncle Bear lost all his hair.

再来看看疑问句，想必相应的发音技巧大家已经非常熟练了：

- What were you thinking?（发音技巧：what 弱读，t 失去爆破，were 弱读，thinking 重读。）
- What was he doing?（发音技巧：what 弱读，t 失去爆破，was 弱读，/z/ 覆盖了 he 中的 /h/ 音并连读。）
- What was she doing?（发音技巧：what 弱读，t 失去爆破，was 弱读后，/z/ 音消失。）
- Was he having fun?（发音技巧：was 弱读，/z/ 覆盖了后面

的 /h/ 音和 he 连读。)

　　• 　Was she doing her best? (发音技巧: was 弱读, /z/ 音被省略, doing 中 "ng" 的音覆盖了 her 中的 /h/ 音并连读。)

　　我们再来看看过去完成时和过去完成进行时。它们的结构分别是: had done, had been doing。

　　其发音技巧和现在完成时、现在完成过去时类似, 只是把 have 变成了 had, 发音技巧中要增加 /d/ 的部分。我们来看下面两个例句:

　　• 　She had done the experiment twice before you came in. 她在你进来之前已经做过两次实验了。

　　• 　By the time you came in, she had been doing the experiment for two hours. 你进来的时候, 她已经做了两个小时的实验了。

　　朗读的时候, 把 had 弱读成 /həd/ 或 "h'd", 然后再根据相应的发音技巧调整就可以了。这两个句子, 你会连读了吗?

　　• 　She h'd done it twice before you came in.

　　• 　By the time you came in, she h'd been doing it for two w hours.

◎ 一般将来时、将来进行时的发音技巧

一般将来时有三种模式，分别是：

be going to…

will do…

be doing…

其中，be going to 和 will do 是常见的一般将来时的表达形式。少数动词可以用 be doing 的形式表示将来要发生的事。比如：

- The bus is coming.
- I'm leaving for Shanghai tomorrow.

这种句子的发音技巧和含有现在进行时的句子用同样的方式处理。我们重点来看 be going to 和 will do。

- I'm going to have dinner with a friend tonight.
- Is he going to have dinner with my sister?
- I will go to New Zealand.
- Will he move to New Zealand?

我们前面接触过，going to 会连读成 gonna，所以前两句会读成：

- I'm gonna have dinner with <u>a</u> friend tonight.
- <u>Is he</u> gonna have dinner with my sister?

注意：初学者在练习 gonna 的发音时，容易犯的错误是在 gonna 后面再加一个 to，一定要记得 gonna 就等于 going to，不要再多此一举！同时，也要注意，除非刻意强调 gonna，一般情况下句子中的 gonna 都会被弱读。

后面两个句子中的难点在于 will 中的 /l/ 音。我们在学音标的时候就能体会到它是个难发标准的音。I will go to... 的句型还比较容易读，但是当 I will 缩写成 I'll 的时候，很多人就会忽视这个 /l/ 的发音了。在最后一句话当中，will he 的 /l/ 吞掉后面的 /h/ 并发生连读，造成了仿佛有两个 /l/ 音的效果，具体如下：

- Will <u>l</u>he move to New Zealand?

◎ 过去将来时、过去将来进行时、过去将来完成时的发音技巧

一般来说，过去将来时态被用到的频率比较少，而经常被用到的是和这些时态长相一模一样的虚拟语气或一些口头上的委婉说法。比如下面的句子：

- I thought I was going to be an actor. 我以为我会成为一个演员。（过去将来时）

- I guess I would choose that one. 我猜我可能会选择那个。（委婉说法，表示假设或猜测）

- If I were you, I would stop being a failure. 如果我是你，我不会再做一个失败者。（虚拟语气）

- Had I been a better man, she wouldn't have left me. 如果我是个更好的人，她就不会离开我了。（虚拟语气）

下面，请大家试着运用各种发音技巧来连读这几句话（这次熊叔没有给出连读的标记，大家可以自己试着用标记法把发音技巧标出来）。

- I thought I was going to be an actor.（过去将来时）

发音技巧：thought 和 I 连读，going to 缩读成 gonna，be 和 an 用 /j/ 的口型滑过，an actor 连读。

- I guess I would choose that one.（委婉说法，表示假设或猜测）

发音技巧：guess 和 I 连读，would 弱读，d 失去爆破，that one 的第二个字母 t 失去爆破。

• If I were you, I would stop being a jerk. (虚拟语气)

发音技巧：if 和 I 连读，would 弱读，d 失去爆破，stop 重读，p 失去爆破，being 和 a 连读。

• Had I been a better man, she wouldn't have left me. (虚拟语气)

发音技巧：had 和 I 连读，同时弱读 had，been 和 a 连读，同时两个词都弱读。wouldn't 的 /n/ 覆盖 /t/，然后继续覆盖后面 have 中的 /h/，和 have 剩下的音连读，同时 have 要弱读。left 的 t 的发音要失去爆破。

由这几个句子，我们再总结一下虚拟语气中常见的弱读现象：

• would have 弱读成 /ˈwədəv/
• wouldn't have 弱读成 /ˈwədn//nəv/

请大家朗读下面两个句子，做连读练习：

• If it hadn't been for you, I would have done a much greater job!
• I wouldn't have done something like that!

最后，在这里附上美剧《老友记》中的一段对话，请大家看完后面熊叔的讲解后，再进行模仿跟读训练。

（大结局）

Monica: Okay, please be careful with that. It was my grandmother's. Be careful.

(Two other men are rolling the big white dog out of the apartment.)

Monica: If that falls off the truck, it wouldn't be the worst thing.

(She slips them some money.)

Ross: Wow.

Rachel: I know. It seems smaller somehow.

Joey: Has it always been purple?

Chandler: (to his children) Look around, you guys. This was your first home. And it was a happy place, filled with love and laughter. But more important, because of rent control, it was a friggin' steal!

(Monica and Chandler put Jack and Erica in their stroller.)

Phoebe: Hey, do you realise that at one time or another we all lived in this apartment?

Monica: Oh, yeah, that's true.

Ross: Uh, I haven't.

Monica: Wait a minute. What about that summer during college that you lived with grandma, and you tried to make it as a dancer?

Ross: Do you realise we almost made it ten years without that coming up?

Monica: Oh, honey, I forgot. I promised Treeger that we'd leave our keys.

Chandler: Oh, okay.

(Chandler and Monica walk over to the kitchen-counter and leave their keys. Then the other four pick out their keys and leave them as well.)

Phoebe: So, I guess this is it.

Joey: Yeah. I guess so.

Monica: (crying) This is harder than I thought it would be.

Chandler: Oh, it's gonna be okay.

(Chandler hugs her. Monica hugs Ross and Rachel as Chandler gets the stroller with the twins.)

Rachel: (crying) Do you guys have to go to the new house right away, or do you have some time?

Monica: We got some time.

Rachel: Okay, should we get some coffee?

Chandler: Sure. Where?

Monica: 好的，这个请小心点。这是我奶奶的（东西）。小心点哦。

（另外两个人正在把那只大白狗推出公寓。）

Monica: 如果那东西从卡车上掉下来，也不是最糟的事儿。

（她偷着给他们塞了点钱。）

Ross: 哇哦。

Rachel: 是啊。不知道为什么，这屋子看上去好像变小了。

Joey: 这屋子一直都是紫色的吗？

Chandler:（对他的孩子说）你们俩多看几眼吧。这是你们的第一个家。这是个幸福的地方，充满了爱和欢笑。但是更重要的是，由于租金管制，这租房的过程简直是经历了一次抢劫！

（Monica 和 Chandler 把 Jack 和 Erica 放到推车里。）

Phoebe: 嘿，你们发现了没？我们都在这个屋子里住过？

Monica: 哦，真的啊，没错。

Ross: 呃，我没有住过。

Monica: 等一会儿。那年夏天你上大学的时候，那会儿你还跟奶奶一起住在这呢吧，那时候你不是还想努力成为一名舞蹈家呢吗？

Ross: 你发现了没？我们几乎有十年成功地没有提及过这件事儿了。

Monica: 哦，对了亲爱的，我忘了个事儿。我答应了 Treeger 我们会把钥匙留下。

Chandler: 哦，好的。

（Chandler 和 Monica 走到厨房柜台那儿，留下了他们的钥匙。然后另外四位也拿出了他们的钥匙并且留在了那儿。）

Phoebe: 所以，我觉得应该就这样了吧。

Joey: 是啊，我觉得也是。

Monica:（哭腔）这比我想象的要难得多。

Chandler: 噢，会好起来的。

（Chandler 抱住她。Monica 拥抱了 Ross 和 Rachel，Chandler 去推双胞胎的婴儿车。）

Rachel:（哭腔）你们俩现在就要去新家那里吗？你们还有时间吗？

Monica: 我们还有时间。

Rachel: 那好，我们一起去喝点咖啡？

Chandler: 好啊。去哪儿？

发音技巧详解（大家可以自己用标注法标记出来）：

Monica: Okay, please be careful with that. It was my grandmother's. Be careful.

发音技巧：第一句中 please、careful、that 重读，be、with 弱读，with 的"th"和后面 that 的"th"合并，发一次音即可。第二句中 it 的字母 t 的发音失去爆破，it was my 都弱读，grandmother's 重读。

Monica: If that falls off the truck, it wouldn't be the worst thing.

　　发音技巧： if 弱读，that 重读，字母 t 的发音失去爆破，接下来 falls off 连读，the 弱读成"th'"，it 和 wouldn't 中的字母 t 的发音失去爆破，同时 it wouldn't be the 四个词全部弱读，worst 中的字母 t 的发音失去爆破。thing 要记得发咬舌音和"大鼻音"。

　　Ross: Wow.

　　发音技巧： 拖慢这个双元音，嘴巴在空中画圈。

　　Rachel: I know. It seems smaller somehow.

　　发音技巧： I know 正常发音即可。it 弱读，t 音省去，smaller 重读，此时可以稍作停顿再说 somehow。

　　Joey: Has it always been purple?

　　发音技巧： has 弱读成"h's"，/z/ 和 it 连读，it 的 t 和 always 连读。

　　Chandler: Look around, you guys. This was your first home.

　　发音技巧： look around 连读。this was your 全部弱读，first 的 /t/ 可以覆盖后面的 /h/，也可以拖长 first，不覆盖后面的 /h/。

　　And it was a happy place, filled with love and laughter.

　　发音技巧： and 只剩下"'n"，和后面的 it 连读，t 的发音失去爆破，was 和 a 连读。前半句可读成：'n i' w' sa happy place. 后半句中 filled 可以选择拖长发音（在用标注法进行标记时，我们可以用"~"来表示拖长发音），这样就不用失去爆破了。后半句可读成：filled~ with love~ 'n laughter。

　　But more important, because of rent control, it was a friggin' steal!

发音技巧：这里其实按照正常的语法规则应该是 more importantly，但是，可能是说话人省略了 what's more important is that 的 what's... is that 吧。句子中，but 肯定要弱读成"b'"，because of 连读，because 可以弱读成"cuz"，rent 中字母 t 发音时失去爆破，it 中字母 t 发音时失去爆破，was 弱读成"w's"，和后面的 a 连读。同时注意到 frigging 在剧本中就直接把后面的 ing 弱读成了 in。

Phoebe: Hey, do you realize that at one time or another we all lived in this apartment?

发音技巧：这里主要需要注意的是朗读过程中的停顿。在 do you realize 这里停顿或者 do you realize that 这里停顿，读句子时 that 可以放在主句中，也可以放在从句中。如果放在从句中，要弱读，并和后面的 at 连读，at 中的字母 t 发音时失去爆破，time 和 or 连读，or 和 another 用卷舌音过渡，we all 用 /j/ 的口型过渡，lived in 按一般过去时的发音规则连读，this apartment 连读，apartment 中间的 t 失去爆破。注意读出升调来。

Monica: Oh, yeah, that's true.

Ross: Uh, I haven't.

Monica: Wait a minute. What about that summer during college that you lived with grandma, and you tried to make it as a dancer?

发音技巧：wait a 连起来读，不要忘记 t 要发成"不送气"的 t。What about 连读，what 的 t 发成"不送气"的 t，about

中的字母 t 发音时失去爆破，that you 可以连读，也可以选择使 that 中的字母 t 发音时失去爆破，lived 中的字母 d 在发音时失去爆破，and you 可以按照 d+j 的读音规则连读，也可以把 and 直接弱读成"'n"，tried 中的字母 d 在发音时失去爆破，make it as a 统统连起来读，其中 it 中的 t 连读后读成"不送气"的 t。dancer 注意发美式发音 / 'dænsɚ/。

Ross: Do you realize we almost made it ten years without that coming up?

发音技巧： do you 弱读，we 弱读，almost 中的字母 t 发音时失去爆破，made it 连读，it 中的字母 t 发音时失去爆破，years 可以适度拖长，without 中的字母 t 发音时失去爆破，这里的 that 不要弱读，字母 t 在发音时失去爆破，coming up 连读。注意读出升调来。

Phoebe: So, I guess this is it.

发音技巧： this is it，全部连起来读。

Joey: Yeah. I guess so.

Monica: This is harder than I thought it would be.

发音技巧： this is 连读，harder 重读，than 弱读成"th'n"，和后面的 I 连读，然后 thought 注意要发咬舌音，t 和 it 连读，it 的 t 失去爆破，would 直接弱读成"w'"。

Chandler: Oh, it's gonna be okay.

7

英语中的
语调训练

　　熊叔一直认为语调跟说话人的说话方式、情绪等有很大的关系。很多同学觉得自己说英语的时候语调很平，那可以反思一下，自己在说母语的时候语调是不是也一样很平，没有起伏和重音呢？练好语调很重要！

　　在训练句子语调的时候，熊叔给大家一个真诚的建议。首先，我们会按照一般规律去划分句子的语调，但是一般规律只是参考，不要把语言学得过于死板。

　　关注微信公众号"熊叔英语"，回复"句子节奏"，收听本章内容的音频讲解以及跟读训练。

◎ 语调的一般规律

　　先来看由一个单词构成的句子和单纯的语气词。

　　对于以下四个词来说，有时候我们会把整个单词的发音拖长，用来表达自己的情绪。

　　1. No! 我们可以拖长，读成 No-oo。这个时候，可以读成降调，No-oo ↓。如果读成升调，则可以表示你是在寻求意见等。

　　2. Yeah! 把发音拖长，读成 Ye-ah。当我们读成降调 Ye-ah ↓ 的时候，可以表示赞同、思考、讽刺等，如果读成升调，可以表示疑问，如"怎么了？""什么事？"等。

3. Hmm… 发音拖长，读成 Hmm-mm，一般表示思考，语气词。大部分时候会读成降调，表示在思考；偶尔升调的时候可以表示疑问，或者"啊？怎么回事儿？"

4. Ah… 发音拖长，读成 Ah…hh，读成降调的时候，表示恍然大悟或者突然想起某件事儿来。升调的时候一般不会拖长发音，会比较干脆地读成"Ah？"表示惊讶、疑惑等。

对于下面这四个由纯语气词构成的"句子"，语调是有讲究的。因为音节多了，所以语调也要配合我们前面学过的重音。

5. Uh huh. 升调的情况比较多，重音在 huh 上，用来表示"同意""我正在听你说""继续继续""没问题"等，很多外国人都喜欢把 uh huh 挂在嘴边。很多时候也会在 uh huh 发音后面加个鼻音，连嘴都不张了，直接闭着嘴哼唧、发出"嗯哼嗯哼"的音。

6. Uh uh. 一般情况下是第一个 uh 重读，然后降调，一般用来表示"不行啊""不可能啊"等。

7. Uh oh. 一般情况下是第一个 uh 重读，并且降调。一般可以用来表示"哎呀，我忘了""我的天哪，大事不妙"或突然见到了不该见到的事情等，可以翻译成"糟糕""不好""完了"等。

8. Ah ha. 一般是第二个 ha 重读，同时降调，语气会比较重。一般表示"我突然有个好想法""我突然想起来了""这个主意不错""被我逮到了吧！"等。

接下来我们来分析句子中的语调。

一般来讲，英语的句子有这么几种语调组合：

1. 升调。一般用于一般疑问句或者有不确定性质的句子中。其实汉语也类似，我们在说"你想吃麻辣烫？"的时候，通常用的都是升调，只不过英语中的语调比汉语更夸张一些。请大家尝试用升调朗读下面的句子：

- You want to go there with me? 你想和我一起去那里？
- Would you like a cup of coffee? 你想要一杯咖啡吗？
- Seriously? 你是认真的？
- Really? Are you kidding me? 真的吗？你不是在逗我？
- Is it raining out there? 外面下雨了？

当然，升调不仅用于带有问题的句子中，说话时用升调的语气也可以用来表示讽刺、反问或表达一些特定的情绪等。比如：

- You just said you wanted to break up with me? (你刚刚说你想要和我分手？) 这句话结尾的地方用升调说出来，会表现出说话者有些困惑，或者愤怒的情绪。

- You are telling me that Uncle Bear has a new girlfriend? (你告诉我熊叔有新的女朋友了？) 这句话用升调说出来，给人的感觉就是并不相信熊叔有女朋友这件事。

2. 降调。一般用于陈述句、感叹句、祈使句、特殊疑问句中。

陈述句，一般就是以句号结尾的句子，用来陈述事情或者讲道理等。比如：

- I saw a magnificent picture in a book about the primeval forest. 我在一本关于原始森林的书中看到了一幅壮丽的图画。
- Money is not evil by itself. 钱本身无罪。
- A bill is just paper with perceived value to obtain other things we value in other ways. 钱只是一张有感知价值的纸，用来获得其他的、我们所珍视的东西的一种方式。
- Evil is trying to buy happiness. 邪恶就是试图购买幸福。

感叹句，一般以感叹号结尾，可以是英语中特有的感叹句结构，也可以是说话人将某个陈述句附有情绪地说出来。比如，最常见的"Oh my God!"我们来看例句：

- What a magnificent picture it is! 多么壮丽的一幅画啊！
- Oh my God! I've been looking for it! 我的天哪！我一直在找它！
- Come on! 拜托！
- You've got to be kidding me! 你在逗我吗！

祈使句，一般不带有人称，句子可以直接以动词开头，表示建议、命令、请求等。

- Let's go together. 让我们一起去吧。
- Help me with this, please. 请来帮帮我。
- Come and play with me. 过来和我一起玩。
- Live and let live. 宽以待人。

特殊疑问句，以疑问词 what、when、why 等开头，一般用来询问信息。一般情况下，特殊疑问句用降调来读。

- What's your last name? 你的姓氏是什么？
- How are you doing? 你还好吗？
- Why are you doing this? 你为什么要这么做？
- When did you meet her? 你是什么时候见到她的？

当然，有时候一般规律是不适用的。比如，这些特殊疑问句，按照一般规律要用降调来读，但读出来总会让人感觉比较严肃。比如，最后一句 When did you meet her? 倘若稍微加点情绪在里面，如想要表达"我很好奇你们什么时候见面的？"完全可以用升调去读。我们要注意不要把语调学死。

3. 先升调，再降调。这种语调用于选择疑问句或者列举事物的句子中。我们来看下面两个例句：

- Would you like a cup of coffee, ↑ or a cup of tea? ↓
- There's a pen ↑ , some books ↑ , a pair of sunglasses ↑ , and an umbrella ↓ in my bag.

　　我们在读一个比较长的句子中，一般来说都会先升调后降调，因为升调会给人一种句子还没说完的感觉，后面好像还有内容。所以这种选择疑问、列举事物的句子基本都会先升调最后降调。注意回答选择疑问句时应直接回答选择的内容，不要回答 Yes 或者 No。我们来看下面几个例句：

- So, do you want to go back home now ↑ , or spend some more time here? ↓
- I'm going to America! I'll go to New York ↑ , LA, ↑ San Francisco, ↑ and New Orleans! ↓
- I've been to Thailand, ↑ Japan, ↑ France, ↑ Spain, ↑ America, ↑ and Mexico. ↓
- You want to help me ↑ or not? ↓

　　4. 先降调，后升调。这种语调一般用于反义疑问句中，例如小时候家长教训我们的时候经常会说："你还不怕我了，是吧？"这个"是吧？"在英语当中，就是反义疑问句。另外，反义疑问句也可以用 right、yeah 之类的常用词代替。我们来看例句：

- You are not afraid of him ↓ , are you? ↑
- Uncle Bear is a good teacher ↓ , isn't he? ↑
- You don't think you can do this ↓ , right? ↑
- This is gonna work ↓ , yeah? ↑

一般来讲，当你已经说完一件事，后面想提问或者寻求一下别人的建议的时候，都可以先降调、再升调的语气。

5. 先降调，再降调。这种语调同样用于反义疑问句中。在"先降调，后升调"的语调规律中，反义疑问句是用来征求意见或者有提问的，往往有想要得到肯定回复的期望。而当反义疑问句先降调、再降调的时候，则会有种想要表达"就是这样的，不接受反驳"或者"你不会连……都……"的意思在里面，一般情况下不需要对方回复，仅用于加强语气。比如，上面的四个例句，如果用先降调、再降调的方式读出来，表达的意思就完全变了……

- You are not afraid of him ↓ , are you? ↓ （你不会连他都害怕吧！）
- Uncle Bear is a good teacher ↓ , isn't he? ↓ （熊叔是个好老师，事实就是这样的。）

- You don't think you can do this ↓ , do you? ↓（别闹了，你不行的。）
- This is gonna work ↓ , yeah. ↓（没问题的，上吧。）

　　有些时候，我们会用反义疑问句自言自语，这个时候往往也是用先降调、再降调的方式。比如，外面风特别大，你站在窗前冷笑一声自言自语道：

- It's a bit windy out there, ↓ isn't it? ↓

　　用先降调、再降调的方式来说出这句话，会充分体现出说话者的寂寞感。

　　了解了语调的一般规律后，我们不要忘记熊叔之前强调的那句话：语调是很灵活的，不能把语调学死了。下面我们来分析一些常见的句子，配合着不同的重音，感受一下不同的语调带来的不同效果。

　　1. Hello.（降调时，表示打招呼、回应对方等；升调时表示"谁啊？""谁在那儿呢？""你找谁啊，我认识你吗？"等。）

　　2. Good morning.（升调时，会让人觉得说话者精力充沛、心情不错；降调时，就是普通的打招呼，或者回应别人。）

　　3. Really？（降调时，可以表示"你一定是在逗我""我早就知道会这样""我一点也不惊讶"等；升调时，可以表示"哦，天哪，真的吗？""简直太棒了！""你别胡说了，马上我就反驳你。"等。可以看到，同样的语调也可以有不同的语气，可以表现出不同的情绪。）

4. Don't worry about that.（按照一般规则，应该是降调，但是你也可以用升调说出来。升调时，把重音放在 don't 和 that 上，然后在 that 这里上扬语调，表示说话人很放松、温柔，带有亲切或鼓励的语气。）

5. Come on!（这个句子就特别灵活了，可以重读 come，也可以重读 on。重读 come 并且降调时可以表示"别闹了""拉倒吧""赶紧吧""没时间了"等，重读 on 并且升调时，也可以表示"赶紧吧""没时间了""来呀"等。其实只有 come on 两个词的时候，重读 come 基本就是降调了，重读 on 基本就是升调了。）

6. Good luck.（读这个句子时既可以升调也可以降调。升调时表示说话者有点依依不舍，或者实在不知道说什么好了；降调时则可以表示坚定地祝福对方，或者离别的伤感等。）

从以上几个句子可以看出，有些句子，可以配合不同的重音和语调来表达不同的意思和情绪。这就要求我们在训练的过程中，多听原声、多模仿，模仿的同时也要注意模仿原声的"神色"，这个"神色"就是说话者的重读、语调、语气等，这些内容整合起来就是每个句子的"灵魂"。我们在模仿的时候，要尽可能地去揣摩说话者可能会有的心理活动，看看每句话除了字面信息，是否还有些蕴含在句子"灵魂"中的没有通过文字表达出来的信息。一定要记住语调是很灵活的，哪怕是"Would you like a cup of coffee, or a cup of tea?"这样的一句话，如果说话者当时特别疲惫，或者特别烦躁，也会用"Would you like a cup of coffee, ↓ or a cup of tea? ↓"这样的降调方式表达出来。

　　另外，在练习的时候，熊叔建议大家要用比平常正常对话时更夸张一些的语气来读句子。比如，正常对话时"You want a cup of coffee? ↑"那么我们在训练的时候可以把语速放慢，让语调更夸张一些，读成"You~ want a cup of coffee~ ↑？"

　　接下来，请大家大声朗读下面的句子。尝试把自己当成一个演员，按照括号里的要求去演绎这些句子。

- Uncle Bear is only 19 years old. 熊叔只有 19 岁。
- ★ 分别用最惊讶的（↑）和最愤怒的（↓）语气说出来。
- I really miss you. 我真的好想你。
- ★ 分别用最烦躁的（↓）和最伤感的（↑）语气说出来。
- I can't believe she's gone. 我不敢相信她已经走了。
  分别用最苦闷的（↓）和最开心的（↑）语气说出来。
- I'm really excited about it. 我真的很兴奋。
- ★ 分别用最讽刺的（↓）和最兴奋的（↑）语气说出来。
- I told you it wouldn't work. 我告诉过你这行不通的。
- ★ 分别用最冷漠的（↓）、最气愤的（↓）、最悲伤的（↓）、最无奈的（↓）语气说出来。

◎ 当句子很长时，语调该怎么分配？

当我们需要说的或者朗读的句子很长的时候，我们该如何去处理语调呢？一般来说，如果是一个很长的陈述句，前面会采取平调或者升调，最后再降调。比如下面一句话：

- I had thought about living with my grandparents when my parents went abroad last year. 我父母去年出国时，我考虑过和我的祖父母一起住。

如果说话者的语速比较快，那么可以处理成：

- I had thought about living with my grandparents ↑ when my parents went abroad last year. ↓

或者：

- I had thought about living with my grandparents → when my parents went abroad last year. ↓

如果说话者的语速比较慢，也可以多一些语调的起伏。比如：

· I had thought about　→ living with my grandparents　↑
when my parents went abroad ↑ last year. ↓

句子前面的平调或者升调一般也会进行拖长的处理，即：

· I had thought about~ → living with my grandparents~ ↑
when my parents went abroad~ ↑ last year. ↓

如果是一个很长的问句，也用同样的方式处理，前面可以平
调或升调，最后再升调即可。比如：

· If you don't have any plans this weekend, would you like
to watch a movie with me? 如果你这周末没有安排，你愿意和我
一起去看一场电影吗？

如果说话者语速比较快，那么可以处理成：

· If you don't have any plans this weekend,　→ would you
like to watch a movie with me? ↑

当然，类似的提建议的句子也可以把结尾处理成降调。比如：

• If you don't have any plans this weekend, → maybe you and I, ↑ we could watch a movie together. ↓ （↑也完全可行，把句号改成问号即可）

在练习长句子的语调时，最好用的素材就是"VOA Special English"，"VOA 特别英语"，或者"VOA 慢速英语"。VOA 全称为 *Voice Of America*，中文名为《美国之声》，提供一系列的"Special English"节目，大多是新闻、专题等内容，专门向全世界的英语学习者开放，利用百度网站能搜索到很多学习资料。这类节目用词简单，适合有一定基础的英语学习者，语速非常缓慢，抑扬顿挫非常明显，所以非常适合用来练习语调。VOA 大概是什么样的风格呢？请扫描本章二维码收听熊叔录制的示范音频：

This is Uncle Bear with the VOA Special English education report.

Private colleges and universities are growing in popularity around the world. One-third of all higher education students worldwide take classes at such schools. That finding is from a study published earlier this year in the journal Higher Education.

译文：

这里是熊叔带来的美国之声慢速英语教育报道。

私立学院、大学在全世界越来越受欢迎。全世界接受高等教育的学生中有三分之一的学生在这样的学校上课。这项研究来自今年早些时候在《高等教育》期刊上发表的一篇文章。

由于语速非常慢，所以显得停顿非常多，同时语调的变化也就更多。这一小段内容就可以读成：

This ↑ is ↓ Uncle → Bear ↓↑ with the V → O → A ↓↑ Special English ↓ education report. ↓

Private colleges ↑ and universities ↓ are growing in popularity ↑ around the world. ↓ One-third of all higher education students worldwide ↑ take classes at such schools. ↓ That finding ↓↑ is from a study ↑ published earlier this year ↑ in the journal ↓↑ Higher Education. ↓

虽然语速很慢，但却能让人耐心地听下去，这就是语调的魅力。当你把上面一段话练得非常熟练时，你可以把语速变成正常语速，这个时候把自己读的内容录下来听一听，来感受自己发音时语调的变化。

◎ 句子节奏

其实句子节奏是个大杂烩。你可以把一句话唱出来，这是一种节奏，rap（说唱）出来又是一种节奏；像新闻播音员一样"播"出来是一种节奏，像奥巴马一样演讲出来又是一种节奏；平日里和朋友们对话是一种节奏，逗孩子读故事又是一种节奏。那么，节奏到底是怎样的呢？

节奏其实包含了连读、重读、弱读、语调、语速、语气、停顿等。大家看看刚才熊叔列举的内容，是不是就差一个停顿没学了？下面，我们就来学一下句子中的断句。

来看例句：

It was one of the queer things of life that you saw a person every day for months and were so intimate with him that you could not imagine existence without him.

英语中，有的句子会很长，遇到这样的句子，便需要做断句处理。我们在读长句的时候，一般选择在断句的地方停顿。因此，一定要学会停顿的技巧。

断句分为两种方式：第一种，按照意群划分来断句；第二种，按照说话人的意图来断句。类似于我们前面学重读或语调，第一种是一般规律，第二种以人的主观情绪为主要依据。

我们来看第一种断句：按照意群划分。意群，按照字面意思理解，就是表达同一个意思的群体，这个群体自然就是单词、词组、短句、从句等。我们可以把句子按意思和结构划分出各个细小的成分来，每一处成分就代表一个意群。每种语言都有意群，意群对理解句子以及断句意义重大，就像汉语里，很简单的"我是中国人"都可以细分出意群来：我，是，中国人。那么这句话就可以读作：

（在标注法中，我们在这里用 / 来表示停顿）

我 / 是 / 中国人。

我是 / 中国人。

中国人是一个意群，所以这个句子肯定不能读成：我是中 / 国人。

英语也是同样的原则，我们来看几个简单的句子：

- I don't think you can do it.
- Do you want to come to my place for dinner tomorrow night?
- I plan to go to Australia next year.
- It has been raining for at least three days now.

这些比较简单的句子一般来说不用停顿也是可以脱口而出的，但是在特定的场合下，也可以加入一些停顿。

第一句的意群可以划分成 I don't think 和 you can do it。理解为"我不认为"+"你能做到"。

第二句的意群可以划分成 Do you want to（to 也可以划分到后面），come to my place，for dinner，tomorrow night。理解为"你想不想"+"来我这儿"+"吃晚饭"+"明天晚上"。

第三句的意群可以划分成 I plan to（to 也可以划分到后面），go to Australia，next year。理解为"我打算"+"去澳大利亚"+"明年"。

第四句的意群可以划分成 It has been raining，at least，for three days，now。其中 at least 插入 for three days 里面，所以也可以放在一起，组成一个稍微大点的意群，for at least three days。理解为"一直在下雨"+"至少三天"+"到现在"。

如果对意群没能理解透彻，那么对句子的理解就有可能出现偏差。请看下面几个句子：

- Whoever's doing this is certainly not a friend of ours.
- What I'm looking at is not your business.
- I just got yelled at for something I didn't do.

第一句中，有个小从句，如果意群没有划分好，你可能会把 this is 划分到一处去，那你对这个句子的理解就会出现问题，同时读出来的节奏也会错。我们把这个句子划分成两个大的意群，那么将 Whoever's doing this 放在一起理解，相当于主语，然后才是 is certainly not a friend of ours。理解为"不管是谁在做这件事"＋"肯定不是我们的朋友"。

第二句和第一句的节奏类似，What I'm looking at 作主语，另外一处意群是 is not your business。理解为"我在看啥"＋"关你什么事"。

第三句是个被动语态的句子，平时我们在说 yell 的时候，一般都会加上 yell at。比如，The boss is yelling at me again 等。在第三个例句中，"I"是"被吼"的对象，保留了 at，所以 I just got yelled at 为一个意群，而 for something I didn't do 是另一个意群。理解为"我刚刚被吼"＋"因为一些我没做过的事儿"。

另外，大家有没有注意到，第一句中的 this 和 is 没有连读，第二句中的 at 和 is 没有连读，第三句中的 at 中的字母 t 发音时也没有失去爆破，这是为什么？原因很重要，请大家记住：

当句子中需要停顿的时候，是不需要连读的。

- Whoever's doing this（这里停顿）is certainly not a friend of ours.
- What I'm looking at（这里又停顿）is not your business.

所以连读等发音技巧掌握熟练后，也要看看句子中是不是有需要停顿的地方。如果需要停顿，就不用再连读了。

大家可以看到，意群不仅可以帮助我们更好地把握句子的节奏，它也能帮助我们更好地理解句子。在阅读的时候，如果你能把意群作为单位去阅读，你的阅读速度也能得到提高。你可以从小的意群开始阅读，然后慢慢扩大到大的意群。

当句子比较长时，我们首先要对句子的结构有清晰的认识。倒不是要求你详细地划分句子成分，但是你需要做到的是，能够判断出句子中的这些"块状成分"。这些成分个体就可以是意群，每个意群里的词都要连在一起读。你可以把一个句子想象成一棵树，那么树叶就是单词，树枝就是意群，每个意群上有哪些叶子，这些叶子就要被划分到一起。比如上面的第一句：

- Whoever's doing this is certainly not a friend of ours.

我们划分出了 whoever's doing this 和 is certainly not a friend of ours 两个意群。

句子越复杂越需要我们清晰地识别出这些单词分别属于哪个意群。熊叔在本章的最后会向大家介绍一个分析长难句的办法（适合基础很好的同学，基础薄弱的同学就先不要挑战长难句了），让你既能自由分析、彻底理解长难句，也能把长难句顺畅朗读出来。

接下来，我们看第二种断句：按照说话者的意图进行断句。除了常规的停顿需要外，停顿还有哪些其他意义呢？举个简单的例子：假设你在教室里听课，老师不停地讲，而你却听得昏昏欲睡，这个时候老师突然停顿了 10 秒钟，你会有什么反应？

我们一起来看几个句子：

- Uncle Bear, I think you are a terrible person. 熊叔，我觉得你是个糟糕的人。
- Uncle Bear, I was thinking maybe we could go to dinner together tonight. 熊叔，我想也许我们今晚可以共进晚餐。
- Uncle Bear, I've got good news! You just won a million dollars! 熊叔，我有个好消息！你刚刚赢得了一百万美元！

每个句子其实都不需要停顿。但是如果在某些地方加上停顿的话，便会有一些不一样的效果。比如：

第一句我们这样来做停顿：

- Uncle Bear, I think / you are a terrible / person.

两处停顿前的 think 和 terrible 都重读。think 这里做停顿，可以引起 Uncle Bear 的注意，加上一定的语气，可以让 Uncle Bear 对这句话后面的内容有一定的预期。第二处停顿，按照一般规律 a terrible person 应该是一个意群不应该做停顿的，但是这里的停顿加上 terrible 的重读，此处大力强调了"terrible"一词。

第二句，我们如果这样来停顿：

- Uncle Bear, I was thinking / maybe we could / go to dinner / together / tonight.

第一处 thinking 这里的停顿，同样可以引起 Uncle Bear 的注意，并且让 Uncle Bear 对你想说的内容产生了一定的预期。第二处 could 这里的停顿，可以表示说话者在思考，也可以是暗示 Uncle Bear，"we could do something, you know"。dinner 这里的停顿，可以是引起 Uncle Bear 的思考，"you wanna go to dinner with me？"together 这里前后都有停顿，明显是在强调"一起"这一含义。

第三句，我们可以这样来停顿：

- Uncle Bear, I've got good news! You just won / a million / dollars!

won 后面停顿，所以 won 和 a 也不需要连读了。million 这里停顿，起到强调的作用。

有些时候，我们在日常对话中可以插入一些表达用来代替需要思考的停顿。比如，"you know""say""uh"等。外国人很喜欢用"you know"，甚至将其当作"口头禅"。

比如：

· How about we, say, have dinner together tomorrow evening?

· I was thinking, you know, if you're free, you know, we could, uh, go and catch a movie together.

但是熊叔建议，这些类似于口头禅一样的插入语，使用时要懂得适可而止，否则会让人听起来很不舒服。

我们来简单总结一下，除了按照意群进行常规停顿外，我们在句子中的停顿往往会起到以下几个作用：

1. 引起听者的注意；

2. 让听者对你将要说的内容产生一定的预期；

3. 引起听者的思考或回忆；

4. 强调你所说的内容；

5. 起到暗示的作用。

大家看看下面几句话，配合不同的重音，你能用不同的停顿方式读出不同的效果吗？

• I could give you a raise, but I'm not sure if I really want to. 我可以给你加薪，但我不确定我是否真的想给你加薪。

• It has been three years since I last saw you. 我已经三年没见到你了。

注意：下面句子中标注的地方，都可以停顿。大家也可以听一听熊叔读的音频，感受一下在朗读过程中不同的停顿方式带来的不同效果。

• I could / give you / a raise, but / I'm not / sure / If I really / want to.

• It has been / three years/ since I / last saw you.

诗歌和演讲稿中往往会有很多停顿，我们来欣赏一小段莎士比亚的十四行诗：

（选自 *Sonnet* 18）

Shall I compare thee to a summer's day?

Thou art more lovely and more temperate.

Rough winds do shake the darling buds of May,

And summer's lease hath all too short a date.

我怎么能够将你比作夏天？

你比夏天更美丽温婉。

狂风将五月的蓓蕾凋残，

夏日的逗留何其短暂。

如果是生活中的正常对话，那这四个句子每个都不用停顿，直接读到标点符号就行了。但是如果想要读得好听、有韵味，那我们就需要加入一些停顿在里面。比如，可以这样停顿：

Shall I compare thee / to a summer's day?

Thou art more lovely / and more temperate.

Rough winds / do shake the darling buds of May,

And summer's lease / hath all too short a date.

加入停顿后再来朗读，立刻就感觉不一样了。

再看一段演讲，大家可以自己先想想怎么停顿比较合适：

（选自马丁·路德·金的 *I Have A Dream*）

I have a dream that one day this nation will rise up, live out the true meaning of its creed, "We hold these truths to be self-evident; that all men are created equal."

I have a dream that one day on the red hills of Georgia the sons of former slaves and the sons of former slave-owners will be able to sit down together at the table of brotherhood.

我梦想有一天，这个国家会站立起来，真正实现其信条的真谛："我们认为这些真理是不言而喻的；人人生而平等。"

我梦想有一天，在佐治亚的红山上，昔日奴隶的后嗣将能够和奴隶主的后嗣坐在一起，共叙兄弟情谊。

演讲词的停顿可能会更夸张一些，因为演讲本身一般来讲语速偏慢，同时演讲所传达的信息都是非常有质量的。另外，演讲的时候多停顿一点，可以防止演讲人口误、说错话等。马丁·路德·金的停顿如下：

I have a dream / that one day / this nation will rise up / and live out the true meaning of its creed /, "We hold these truths / to be self-evident / that all men / are created equal."

I have a dream / that one day / on the red hills of Georgia / the sons of former slaves / and the sons of former slave-owners / will be able to sit down together at the table of brotherhood.

◎ 拖长单词的读音

伴随着句子中的重读、停顿，我们也会选择将一些单词的读音拖长，来达到控制句子节奏的效果。一般来说，重读的单词、停顿前的单词、刻意突出强调的单词都可以进行拖长发音。我们来看下面几个例句：

- That's way too much, man.
- Come and live with me and be my love.
- This is the survival of the fittest.
- You've got to be kidding me.
- You must be really poor.

在用标注法进行标记时，我们可以用"~"来表示拖长发音。上面几句话中可以拖长发音的单词是：

• That's way~ too much, man. 强调并拖长 way 的发音，此处并不需要停顿，用于强调 too much 的程度："太"多了，哥们儿。

• Come and live with me and be~ my love. 强调并拖长 be 的发音，加上适当的停顿，让听者浮想联翩，同时把 my love 重点突出。

• This~ is~ the survival of the fittest. （适者生存）这是歌手 Eminem 演唱的歌曲 Survival 中的一句歌词，this is 的发音都拖长，并且停顿、不连读，起到引起注意、重点突出后面内容的效果。

• You've got~ to be kidding me. 重读并拖长 got 的发音，并且不再和 to 连读，这里起到强调作用，你"一定"是在逗我。

• You must be really~ poor. 重读并拖长 really 的发音。大家可以想象一下，一个身家上亿的老板买了双 200 元的鞋，然后他跟你哭穷说"这鞋太贵了"，然后你对他说这句"You must be really~ poor"，很明显，这里发音的拖长表示反讽。

拖长单词发音的意义很明显，一般是用于强调、引起注意，有时候也可以用来讽刺、吐槽。英语句子中，通过连读、重读、弱读、缩读，配合语调、停顿、单词发音拖长等，就可以大致控制住句子的节奏了。最适合练习控制句子节奏的素材，就是 rap

（说唱）了。下面我们就一起学几句真正的 rap，感受一下：

I can't tell you what it really is

I can only tell you what it feels like

And right now there's a steel knife in my windpipe

I can't breathe but I still fight while I can fight

As long as the wrong feels right it's like I'm in flight

——*Love The Way You Lie*

虽然只有五句话，但是练好可能要半个小时。我们分成每个句子来看：

（下面熊叔用标注法来标记涉及的发音技巧，其中"___"表示连读，在需要表示失去爆破的字母上画短线，如 t，加粗表示重读，"/"表示停顿，"~"表示拖长发音，单词斜体表示弱读等。）

- I **can't**~ / tell you *what* it **really** j is

发音技巧解析：can't 在这里要重读，并且适当拖长发音，同时 t 失去爆破。重读和拖长 can't 除了表示强调外，也为了迎合歌曲节拍。将 tell you 的 l 和 you 连起来，读成"tel lyou"。what 可以弱读，也可以正常读，连读 what 中的字母 t 和 it，注意，这里 what 中的字母 t 要变成"不送气"的 t，it 中的字母 t 要失去爆破。really 重读，和后面的 is 用 /j/ 的口型进行过渡。

- I can only tell you *what* it **feels**~ like

发音技巧解析：整体节奏和上一句差不多，根据伴奏节拍，这次重读了 I 和 feels。

- 'nd right **now**~, *there's* still a **kni**~fe in my **wind**pipe

发音技巧解析：and 基本弱读成了"'n"，right 中的 t 失去爆破，重读 now 并且拖长发音，there's 要弱读，将 still 和 a 连读成"still la"，然后对 knife 的处理要注意一下，knife 拖长发音了，但只是拖长了"kni"的发音，f 的发音与后面的 in 进行了连读，所以是"kni~fin"这样的发音。windpipe 重读第一个音节。

- I can't **breathe**~ b't I still **fight** while I can **fight**

发音技巧解析：I 其实可以做弱读处理，can't 中的字母 t 失去爆破，重读 breathe 并拖长发音，弱读 but，连读 t 和 I，重读两个 fight，第一个 fight 中的字母 t 失去爆破。连读 while 和 I，读成"while li"。

- As **long** as the **wrong**~ feels **right** it's like I'm in **flight**

发音技巧解析：重音放在 long、wrong、right 和 flight 上，因为音节比较多，节奏比较快，所以只是稍微拖长了 wrong 的发音。连读方面，long 和 as 的连读要用到"大鼻音"，难度有些大，right 和 it's 本来属于两个意群，正常说话时可以不连读，不过这里因为节奏紧凑，所以也连在一起读了。like 和 I'm 连读，I'm 中的字母 m 和 in 继续连读。

恭喜大家完成了学习 rap 的第一步——把歌词读顺。接下来，需要大家对照着歌曲的伴奏反反复复地听，熟悉歌曲的节奏，然后继续往下练。后面我们会有一个专门的部分来讲解如何学习英文 rap，有助于大家更熟练地掌握英文发音的节奏。

◎ 语速的意义

最后来说一下语速。语速其实是更倾向于由个人习惯所决定的，但是有些时候语速的变化也能起到不同的效果。比如，读那种柔情似水的情诗时，语速不适宜太快，音调不适合太高；在演讲时，语速不适合过快，否则别人会跟不上你的思路；人在情绪比较激动的时候，语速一般就会提升。所以语速相对来说更加灵活。

下面我们来看几个例子，帮助大家调整自己的语速，让自己的表达更有表现力（以下两段话均出自美剧 *Friends*）。

- You've gotta just keep thinking about the day that some kid is gonna run up to his friends and go, "I got the part! I got the part! I'm gonna be Joey Tribbiani's ass!" (乔伊演替身被辞退，非常沮丧。菲比在安慰他) 你得一直想着，总有一天会有某个小孩跑去找他的朋友说："我得到了这个角色，我得到了这个角色，我将要演乔伊·崔比尼的屁股。"

- I told everybody about this! Now everybody's gonna go to the theatre, expecting to see me, and... 我已经跟所有人说了！现在每个人都会去电影院，希望看到我，而且……

这两句话中，加速的部分熊叔用"（　）"标出来，如下：

- (You've gotta just) keep thinking (about the day that some) kid (is gonna run up to his friends and go,) ("I got the part! I got the part! I'm gonna be Joey Tribbiani's ass!")

- I told everybody about this! (Now everybody's gonna go to the theatre, expecting to see me, and)...

简单来讲，平日对话时，语速加快一般有两种情况：

1. 加速的部分在句子当中并不关键或者信息量很小。比如，第一句中的 (You've gotta just)，(about the day that some)，(is gonna run up to his friends and go)。

2. 当我们语速加快时，往往是因为我们处于激动、兴奋等状态。比如，第一句中的 ("I got the part! I got the part! I'm gonna be Joey Tribbiani's ass!") 和第二句中的 (Now everybody's gonna

go to the theatre, expecting to see me, and...）。

与之相反，句子中重要的部分，即需要我们进行强调的内容，我们就会（相对来讲）放慢语速。当我们想展现我们的温柔、淡定、放松等状态时，也会放慢语速。另外，针对特殊情况，如演讲、诗朗诵等，一般也会用相对较慢的语速。

大家可以观察一下熊叔讲课时的风格，当涉及要讲的重点时，语速一定是相对放慢的。

大家在练习口语、发音的过程中也要记住，先从尽可能慢的语速练起，然后一点一点地加快语速。

可以说，本章所讲的所有内容，配合前面的连读等发音技巧，共同构成了句子的节奏。想把句子说得很有"美国味儿"，不是一件简单的事儿，但只要你能把熊叔这本书中所讲的要点都掌握，并勤加练习，相信在两三个月的时间内，你就会取得非常大的进步。从下一章开始，我们进入包含全部发音技巧和句子节奏把控的综合训练。

◎ 长难句的解剖方法

It will never be known how and when this numeration ability developed, but it is certain that numeration was well developed by the time humans had formed even permanent settlements.

乍一看这句话，哪怕你是英语基础不错的同学也会觉得复杂。

不过别慌，熊叔告诉大家，这样的句子只要简单的几步，我们就可以掌握它的精髓了！

首先，看到长难句后要做的第一件事就是去找句子中的动词，然后对句子结构进行分解。

例如：

It will never **be known** how and when this numeration ability **developed**, but it is certain that numeration **was** well **developed** by the time humans **had formed** even permanent settlements.

当你把动词都找出来之后，句子就可以顺着这些动词进行分解了。我们把每个动词所在的位置梳理一下：

- It will never **be known**…
- how and when this numeration ability **developed**…
- but it **is** certain that…
- numeration was well **developed**…
- by the time humans **had formed** even permanent settlements.

根据动词所在的位置，这个句子被拆成了这五个部分，接下来，我们要做的就是针对这五个部分，找出句子的主干。找句子主干的时候，我们主要看的是句子中哪些部分是作为信息存在的，哪些部分是作为功能存在的。这些作为信息存在的地方，我们就可以想个办法把它简化掉。

It will never **be known**…这部分没有提供什么具体的信息，完全是功能性结构。how and when this numeration ability **developed**…这部分是一段信息（我们甚至都不用知道具体信息是什么）。

but it is certain that… 和第 1 部分类似，是功能性结构。

numeration **was** well **developed**… 这部分仍然在说"numeration"这件事，是一段信息。

by the time humans **had formed** even permanent settlements，关键词 time 告诉我们这部分是关于时间的信息。

至此，句子的主干就非常清晰了。我们把功能性结构保留，把信息结构用字母 A、B、C 代替，句子结构为：

It will never be known A, but it is certain that B (by the time) C. 这回句子很容易懂了吧？翻译过来就是，A 永远不会被人知道，但是可以确信的是，在 C 这个时间之前，B 发生了。

A=how and when this numeration ability **developed**，查字典得知 numeration 的意思是"计算、计数"，我们一看这个词的长相就能知道跟数字 number 有关系。那么 A= 这个计数能力是在什么时候以及如何开发出来的。

B=numeration **was** well **developed**，B= 计数能力已经发展得相当好了。

C=by the time humans **had formed** even permanent settlements. 查词典得知 permanent settlement 的意思是长期居住、永久定居等，那么 C= 当人类已经形成永久的定居模式时（之前），把 A、B、C 带回句子当中就有了这样的理解：

（这个计数能力是在什么时候以及如何开发出来的）永远不会

被人知道，但是可以确信的是，（当人类已经形成永久的定居模式之前），（计数能力已经发展得相当好了）。

虽然有些地方的翻译还需完善，但是理解这句话已经不成问题了吧？如果你的目的仅仅是理解句子，那到这里就已经足够了。当然，你还可以继续把翻译按照我们的习惯去改善一下，这里就比较考验你的语文水平了。比如，你可以把它译为：

人们永远不会知道这种计数能力是如何以及何时开发的，但可以确定的是，当人类形成永久的定居模式之前，这种计数能力就已经非常发达了。

找动词，分解句子结构，用字母 A、B、C 代替其中的信息结构，总结出句子主干，然后再用字母 A、B、C 理解句子。这样对长难句进行了彻底的剖析后，其实，我们的句子节奏也已经划分出来了。如果我们不能完全理解句子，那断句便不会准确，更别说能读得好听了。刚刚的这个句子如果一上来就直接读，那会读得很累，因为你不知道怎么断句。但是当你分析完句子结构之后，就可以很自然地进行断句了。

It will never be known / how and when this numeration ability developed, / but it is certain / that numeration was well developed / by the time humans had formed even permanent settlements.

我们再来练习一个句子，尝试用这种方法来剖析句子的结构。

From earliest childhood we are so bound up with our system of numeration that it is a feat of imagination to consider the problems faced by early humans who had not yet developed this facility.

首先，From earliest childhood we <u>are</u> <u>so</u> bound up with our system of numeration <u>that</u>，这部分当中比较特殊的地方是句子里有 so... that 这样的结构，意思是如此……以至于……，所以我们可以把这里的主干提炼为：...we are so A that...，然后剩下的部分再单独来分析。

其次，...it is a feat of imagination to consider the problems faced by early humans who had not yet developed this facility. 这里按照上面所说的方法就可以了。如果你不熟练，可以分得更细致一些。比如：

It is B to consider C faced by D who had not yet E.

如果你足够熟练，可以把很多小部分合并在一起，如：

It is B to consider C.

于是整个句子被剖析成：

(Time) we are so A that it is B to consider C.

从……开始，我们就如此地 A，以至于当我们考虑 C 的时候是 B 的。

time 等同于 from earliest childhood。

A=bound up with our system of numeration，查词典发现，be bound up with 意为"与……关系密切"，那么 A 可以理解为：我们和我们的计数系统关系密切。

B=a feat of imagination，feat 意为"壮举"，feat of imagination 意为"想象的壮举"，也就是我们需要尽可能地发挥想象力才能想象到的事儿。

C=the problems faced by early humans who had not yet developed this facility，如果你不熟练，这个部分还需要进一步分析。大致可以理解为：早先的还没有开发出计数能力的人们所面对的问题。

回到原句当中：

从（初期的童年）开始，（我们就和我们的计数系统）如此密切，以至于当我们考虑（早先的还没有开发出计数能力的人们所面对的问题）时，（需要我们尽可能地发挥想象力）。

到这里，虽然我们的翻译还需完善，但是你肯定已经理解了这句话的意思。把翻译稍作加工，我们可将其译为：从小开始，我们的生活就和计数密切相关，所以我们要绞尽脑汁才能想象出那些还没有计数能力的先人们所面对的问题。

我们也可以尝试断句后再朗读这个句子：

From earliest childhood /we are so bound up with our system of numeration that / it is a feat of imagination / to consider the problems faced by early humans / who had not yet developed this facility.

通过剖析长难句，我们不仅深刻地理解了句子，也能更流畅地读出这些句子。简单总结一下，在剖析长难句的过程中，需要注意以下几点：

1. 不要纠结小问题，要去理解大的结构。比如，当你看到长难句的时候，就不要去想"这个介词为啥是 at 而不是 in""这个冠词为啥不是 the 而是 a"这种问题了，一定要先关注句子的结构。

2. 不要因为个别单词而阻碍你对整个句子的理解，句子结构仍然最重要。遇到不会的单词就先放着，句子结构剖析完之后，再查词典学习这些不懂的词汇，所以一切以句子结构为主。

既使有很多单词不认识，你也完全不用慌，因为这并不妨碍对句子结构的分析，那些陌生单词的发音和释义的问题通过查词典都可以解决。

3. 在我们理解了句子的含义之后，我们要开始朗读句子了。朗读的时候，根据自己的情况来划分停顿的位置和停顿的数量。如果你很熟练，就少停顿几处，把多个意群合并成一个大意群；如果你很陌生，就多停顿，语速慢一点，练熟了之后再去掉一些不必要的停顿。慢慢你会发现，如果一个人能很熟练、流利地朗读长难句，那他对句子的理解也一定是很到位的。

4. 刚接触长难句时，不管是分析句子还是朗读句子，难度都很大。随着我们的积累和练习，大脑对长难句的理解会越来越熟练，慢慢地你就能到达"看一遍句子就能断好句读出来"的境界了，练习的过程中要有耐心。

5. 想把长难句读好，也需要大家的英语达到一定的水平。基础差的、甚至零基础的同学就不要挑战长难句了。

8
CHAPTER

地道美音
综合训练

本书讲到这里，美式发音的技巧便介绍完了。下面，我们针对不同的题材，来开启美式发音的综合训练。在开始练习之前，不妨回到本书的开头，回顾一下熊叔给大家介绍的各种练习方法！

关注微信公众号"**熊叔英语**"，回复"**美音综合训练**"，收听本章内容的音频讲解以及跟读训练。

◎ 日常对话

（素材均改编自教材 *Top Notch* 第二册）

这种日常的小对话非常适合我们做发音练习。选自教材的对话一般语速控制得当，不会像英国人或美国人正常说话时那样有很快的语速（参考美剧《老友记》或《摩登家庭》等），同时根据所选教材的等级，知识点比较集中，词汇量也控制得很好。在练习此类对话时，建议大家先多听几遍，如果你对各个发音技巧很熟练，就先自己试着朗读，然后再跟读。如果你对各个发音技巧还不是很熟练，建议大家先用标记法把相关的发音技巧标记出来，然后用非常慢的语速去练习。

第一组

Uncle Bear: You look familiar. Haven't we met somewhere before?

熊叔：你看着挺眼熟的，我们之前是不是在哪儿见过？

Taka: I don't think so. I'm not from around here.

塔卡：没有吧，我不是这的。

Uncle Bear: I remember! Aren't you from Japan? I'm sure we met at the IT conference last week.

熊叔：我想起来了。你是从日本来的吧？我们肯定在上周的那个 IT 会议上见过。

Taka: Of course! You're from Mexico, right?

塔卡：对啦！你来自墨西哥，对吧？

Uncle Bear: No, I'm from China. I'm sorry, I've forgotten your name.

熊叔：不是，我来自中国。不好意思啊，我忘记你的名字了。

Taka: Kamura Takashi. But you can call me Taka.

塔卡：我叫 Kamura Takashi。你可以叫我塔卡。

Uncle Bear: Hi, Taka. Uncle Bear. So, what have you been up to since the conference?

熊叔：塔卡，你好啊！我是熊叔。那么，会议之后你都忙什么了呢？

Taka: Not much. Actually, I'm on my way to the airport now. I'm flying back home.

塔卡：也没忙些什么。其实，我现在正要去机场。我要回国了。

Uncle Bear: Hey, we should keep in touch. Here's my card. The conference is in Tieling next year, and I could show you around.

熊叔：哦，我们应该保持联系。这是我的名片。明年的会议会在铁岭举办，我可以带你四处逛逛。

Taka: That would be great. I hear Tieling is beautiful.

塔卡：那太好了。我听说铁岭很美。

Uncle Bear: It was nice to see you again, Taka.

熊叔：塔卡，能再见着你真是太好了。

Taka: You, too.

塔卡：我也是。

美音小贴士：

· Haven't we met somewhere before? 这句话的语调很灵活，可以先降调再升调，也可以先升调再升调。

· I'm not from around here. 这句话中的 around here 有几种处理方式：你可以按照拼写正常读 around here，也可以把 around 中的字母 d 的发音失去爆破，读作 around here，还可以把字母 h 的发音省掉，读成 "around ere".

· Aren't you from Japan? 不要忘记 aren't you 中 t 和 y

要连读。

• We met at the IT conference… 这里的 the 发音会变成 /ði/，因为后面的单词 IT 是元音开头。对话后面的 the airport，airport 也是元音开头，所以 the 发音同样要变成 /ði/。另外注意，the 在重读的时候也会读成 /ði/。

• So, what have you been up to since… 这句话中，重读的只有 up to，所以 what have you been 都应该弱读，what have 直接弱读成 "wh't've"。

• Hey, we should keep in touch. 这句话中的 should 会做弱读处理，读成 "sh'd"。包括后面的 I could show you around 和 That would be great 等，could 和 would 都会弱读成 "c'd" 和 "w'd"。

• That would be great. 可以正常读，把 That would be 三个词都弱读。也可以把 That 单独突出出来，进行重读和拖长发音，并加入停顿。That~ would be great，这样说出来，听上去会让人觉得你真的在思考这件事。

• It was nice to see you again… 这里的 it、was、to、you 都要弱读，分别读成 "i" "w's" "t" "ye"。

第二组

Uncle Bear: Didn't you tell me you were avoiding sweets?

熊叔：你不是说不吃甜食了吗？

Aunt Bear: I couldn't resist! I had a craving for chocolate.

熊婶儿：我抵挡不了它的诱惑，我特别爱吃巧克力。

Uncle Bear: Well, I have to admit it looks pretty good. How many calories are in that thing anyway?

熊叔：嗯，我也承认，巧克力看上去是挺诱人的。你说巧克力里包含多少卡路里啊？

Aunt Bear: I have no idea. Want to try some?

熊婶儿：我也不知道。你想尝尝吗？

Uncle Bear: Thanks. But I think I'd better pass. I'm avoiding carbs.

熊叔：谢谢，但是我还是别吃了。我现在不吃含碳水化合物的食物。

Aunt Bear: You? I don't believe it. You never used to turn down chocolate!

熊婶儿：你吗？我可不信。你从来没有拒绝过巧克力。

Uncle Bear: I know. But I'm losing my weight now.

熊叔：我也知道啊。但是我目前在减肥。

Aunt Bear: Come on! It's really good.

熊婶儿：来尝尝吧，真的很好吃。

Uncle Bear: OK. Maybe just a bite.

熊叔：好吧，那就整一小口。

Aunt Bear: Hey, you only live once!

熊婶儿：嘿，人生得意须尽欢！

美音小贴士：

• Didn't you tell me you were avoiding sweets? 句子中的 didn't you 要记得 t 和 y 连读。当然，也有另外一种处理方式，就是用 n 的发音覆盖后面的 t 的发音，读成 "didn' you"。语调可以先降后升。

• I had a craving for chocolate. 可以选择把 craving 的发音拖长。

• I have to admit it looks pretty good. 这里可以在 admit 和 it 之间加入停顿，就无须连读了。如果你语速较快，也可以直接连读。

• Want to try some？读成 Wanna try some？

• You never used to turn down chocolate! 这句话中一定要重读 never，其他都可以不重读。

• But I'm watching my weight now. 注意 but 弱读成 "b't"，t 和 I 连读，同时要注意这里的 t 读作 "不送气" 的 t。

• It's really good. 这句话里可以通过重读和拖长发音的方式来强调 really。

• Hey, you only live once! 这句话中的 only、live、once 几个词都可以单独重读。可以放慢语速，一词一顿地去读。结尾可以把声调上扬，让句子更有活力。

第三组

Matt: I can't believe it! I just picked this up to look at it and the thing broke in two. And with these ridiculous prices, it's going to cost me an arm and a leg.

马特： 我简直不敢相信，我只是拿起来看了看，它就断成两截了。这东西简直是天价，我可要拿命来赔了！

Uncle Bear: Oh, forget it. I'll bet it was already broken.

熊叔： 哎呀，放那儿吧！我敢打赌它早就坏了。

Matt: You're probably right.

马特： 或许你是对的。

Uncle Bear: Just put it back on the shelf. The place is empty. No one saw. Let's just split.

熊叔： 你就把它放回架子上吧。这个地方都没有人，没人看见。我们赶紧走。

Matt: I couldn't do that.

马特： 我不能那样做。

Uncle Bear: Why not? You said it yourself. The prices are ridiculous.

熊叔： 为什么？你自己都说了，这个东西非常昂贵。

Matt: Well, put yourself in the owner's shoes. Suppose the plate were yours? How would you feel if someone broke it and didn't tell you?

马特： 嗯，假设你是这的老板，而这个东西是你的，如果有人把它弄坏了，然后并没有告诉你，你会有何感想？

Uncle Bear: Well, I'm not the owner. And, anyway, for him it would be just a drop in the bucket. To you, it's a lot of money.

熊叔： 嗯，我不是老板。无论如何，这东西对他来说只是沧海一粟，对你来说，这是一大笔钱。

Matt: Maybe so. But if I ran out without telling him, I couldn't face myself.

马特： 可能吧。但是如果我就这么跑了而不告诉他，我面对不了我自己。

> **美音小贴士：**
>
> 这段对话当中，很多句子中会出现多次连读的现象，建议大家在练习的过程中放慢语速。
>
> • I just picked this up to look at it and the thing broke in two. 可以通过标记法看到有很多处连读，尤其是 look at it and 这里全部都要连起来，需要大家慢慢练习。
>
> • …an arm and a leg. 此处存在多处连读。
>
> • Just put it back on the shelf. 此处既存在连读，也存在失去爆破的发音。
>
> • You said it yourself. 由于 you said it 和 yourself 属于两个小意群，所以 it 和 yourself 可以不连读，把 it 中的字母 t 失去爆破。如果你语速很快，可以把小意群合并，按照我们所学的 t+y 的方式去连读。

- And, anyway, for him it would be... 这里的 for him 后面可以停顿, 同时强调 him。同样, 下一句中的 To you, 强调 you, 并加入停顿。

◎ 绕口令大作战

我们在学习音标的过程中已经体验了绕口令的练习, 作为对某个音标的特别训练。其实绕口令的特性决定了它很适合作为特定音标或发音技巧的训练素材, 下面我们就通过练习以下三组绕口令, 看看它们都在练习哪些音标、哪些发音技巧。

第一组

1. While we were walking, we were watching window washers wash Washington's windows with warm washing water.

当我们走路时, 我们看着清洁窗户的人用温水清洗华盛顿的窗户。

2. Give me the gift of a sock: a drip-drape, ship-shape, and tip-top sock.

给我这双作为礼物的袜子: 悬挂状的、船形的、品质一流的袜子。

3. Betty and Bob brought back blue balloons from the big

bazaar.

Betty 和 Bob 从大杂货店市场上买回来了蓝气球。

4. Susan shines shoes and socks; she ceased shining shoes and socks for shoes and socks shock Susan.

Susan 把鞋子和袜子擦亮，她停止了将鞋子和袜子擦亮，因为鞋子和袜子把 Susan 吓坏了。

5. Chop shops stock chops.

印章店备有印章。

6. Six shimmering sharks sharply striking shins.

六条闪闪发光的鲨鱼猛烈地攻击小腿。

美音小贴士：

1. 第一句中，很明显是在练习 /w/、/ɔ/（walk）、/ɑ/（watch，wash 等）、/ɔr/（warm），通过一个绕口令，把这些易混淆的发音一网打尽。

2. 这句话中主要对比的是：/ɪ/（gift，grip，drip 等）、/e/，/e/ 为美式音标，对应的国际音标是 /eɪ/（drape，shape 等）以及 /ɔ/（top，sock 等）。

3. 这句话中，除了要注意元音的发音外，也要注意 Betty 中的字母 t 要读成"不送气的" t，brought、back 等词中 t、ck 的发音要失去爆破。

4. 这句话主要对比的是 /s/（Susan，socks 等）和 /ʃ/（shines，shoes 等）。

5.这里主要对比 /s/（stock）、/ʃ/（shops）以及 /tʃ/（chop 等）。

6.和第四句类似，这里同样在对比 /s/（six，striking 等）和 /ʃ/（shimmering，sharks 等）。

第二组

1. Don't pamper damp scamp tramps that camp under ramp lamps.

不要纵容潮湿的流浪汉在斜坡灯下扎营。

2. I never felt a piece of felt which felt as fine as that felt felt, when first I felt that felt hat's felt.

在我感受到那个毡帽的手感后，再也没有觉得哪个毛毡的手感和那次感觉到的一样好了。

3. What a shame such a shapely sash should such shabby stitches show！

可惜了这么有型的腰带却搭配那么蹩脚的针法！

4. Thieves seize skis.

小偷们抓住了滑雪板。

5. Whether the weather be fine or whether the weather be not. Whether the weather be cold or whether the weather be hot. We'll weather the weather whether we like it or not.

无论天气是好还是坏，无论天气是冷还是热，无论我们是否喜欢，我们都将适应天气。

美音小贴士：

1. 这里对比了一些辅音，如 /p/（pamper）、/d/（damp）、/tr/（tramps）、/k/（camp）、/r/（ramp）、/l/（lamps）等。另外也练习了爆破音在 /s/ 后面失去爆破的情况，如 /sk/（scamp）。

2. 该例句主要练习了 felt 这个单词的发音，对比了 fine、first 的发音等。

3. 该例句主要还是对比了 /s/（such，sash 等）和 /ʃ/（shame，shapely 等），同时也要注意涉及的连读（如 what a）、失去爆破（如 should such...）等发音技巧。

4. 该例句只有三个词，但是却是熊叔认为的本组最难的绕口令之一。

5. 该例句主要练习了 weather、whether 这两个同音词。

第三组

1. Betty Botter bought some butter, but she said, "this butter's bitter! But a bit of better butter will but make my butter better." So she bought some better butter, better than the bitter butter, and it made her butter better so it was better. Betty Botter bought a bit of better butter!

贝蒂买了些黄油，但是她说："这黄油有点苦。但再买点好黄油就能让我的黄油更好一点。"所以她买了些好黄油，比原来的苦黄油稍好一点的黄油，这使得她的黄油好吃了一些。贝蒂买了一些好黄油。

2. Few free fruit flies fly from flames.

很少有果蝇从火焰中飞过去。

3. Rita repeated what Reardon recited when Reardon read the remarks.

当里尔登读评论时，丽塔重复里尔登背诵的东西。

4. Fifty-five flags freely flutter from the floating frigate.

55 面旗帜在轻轻漂浮的战舰上自由地飘扬。

5. How many sheets could a sheet slitter slit if a sheet slitter could slit sheets?

如果裁纸机能裁纸的话，一个裁纸机能裁多少张纸呢？

6. Ted sent Fred ten hens yesterday so Fred's fresh bread is ready already.

泰德昨天给弗莱德送去了十只母鸡，所以弗莱德的新鲜面包已经准备好了。

美音小贴士：

1. 这一组绕口令很长，但是节奏感很强。除了 Betty、Botter、bought、butter 等单词呈现的不同的元音对比之外，这一组更重要的是爆破音的失去爆破、t 的"不送气"以及连读。只有这样你才能掌握这个绕口令的精髓，实现节奏上的突破。

2. 该例句的难点在于 /f/、/fl/、/fr/ 的饶舌，/l/ 和 /r/ 的发音一定要分清。

3. 该例句对 /r/ 的发音熟练度要求很高。除此之外也要注意句子中 what、when 等词的弱读。

4. 该例句练的是唇齿摩擦音 /f/ 以及 /f/ 和 /l/、/r/ 组合的辅音连缀的发音熟练度。难度和第二个例句差不多。

5. 该例句对比了两组发音，分别是 /s/ 和 /ʃ/ 以及 /ɪ/ 和 /i/（国际音标中的 /i/ 和 /i:/）。同时注意断句，在 could a sheet slitter slit 这里可以停顿，继续接上 if a sheet slitter could…，最后要注意连读爆破音的失去爆破。比如 could 和 a 连读，if 和 a 连读，could slit sheets 中的字母 d 和 t 的发音都失去爆破等。

6. 该例句主要练的是含有 /ɛ/ 音的不同辅音组合的发音。难度不大。

◎ 美剧大作战

（素材选自《老友记》《绝望的主妇》《摩登家庭》等）

原汁原味的美剧是最适合练习发音的素材！但是对学习者的要求较高！你不仅要提前了解本书中熊叔教给大家的所有发音技巧，也需要你有一定的英语基础！毕竟是最地道的素材，没有一定的语言基础是比较难啃下来的。熊叔建议大家在选取美剧（英剧）时，多选取生活场景较多的进行模仿练习。你可以通过下面熊叔总结的美剧七步训练法对所选取的片段先进行听力练习，然后再进行口语模仿练习。

Step 1：对照双语字幕，反复看、听，确保自己能听懂每个单词，知道每个单词的意思。

Step 2：对照英语字幕，反复看、听，确保自己能理解每一分每一秒的信息。

Step 3：对照汉语字幕，反复看、听，确保自己能听出每句话、每个单词来。这个时候，你也可以拿出对话素材来仔细研读一下。

Step 4：无字幕，反复看、听，确保自己能理解每句话，并能听出每个单词来。

Step 5：看字幕或素材，用标记法标记出所有的发音技巧，如果发音技巧熟练，可以省略标记法的步骤。从很慢的语速开始，反复大声朗读，直到可以跟上美剧的速度。

Step 6：把片段静音，尝试自己对照字幕配音。

Step 7：把片段静音，尝试自己在无字幕的情况下进行配音。

第一段（素材选自《老友记》第一季第二集）

情景再现：

Ross 和 Monica 是兄妹。俩人在外闯荡。一天 Ross 和 Monica 的父母前来探望他们。Ross 和 Monica 的父母一直都很喜欢 Ross，认为 Ross 是个完美的儿子，相对而言对 Monica 却经常冷嘲热讽，似乎很不待见 Monica。而此时，Ross 刚刚离婚，他的老婆喜欢女人，而且他老婆怀孕了……

在谈话过程中，Mr. Geller 和 Mrs. Geller，也就是 Ross 和 Monica 的父母，像往常一样把"炮火"对准了 Monica，而 Monica 则对 Ross 说："你跟咱爸妈说说你前妻的事儿，他们就不会一直盯着我吐槽了吧！"

Mrs. Geller: Oh, Martha Ludwin's daughter is gonna call you. (Tastes a snack.) Mmm! What's that curry taste?

Monica: Curry.

Mrs. Geller: Mmmm!

Ross: I- I think they're great! I, I really do.

Mr. Geller: (To Ross) Do you remember the Ludwins? The big one had a thing for you, didn't she?

Mrs. Geller: They all had a thing for him.

Ross: Aw, Mom...

Monica: I'm sorry, why is this girl going to call me?

Mrs. Geller: Oh, she just graduated, and she wants to be something In cooking, or food, or... I don't know. Anyway, I told her you had a restaurant.

Monica: No Mom, I don't have a restaurant, I work in a restaurant.

Mrs. Geller: Well, they don't have to know that... (She starts to fluff the same pillow Monica fluffed multiple times earlier.)

Monica: Ross, could you come and help me with the spaghetti, please?

Ross: Yeah. (They go to the kitchen.)

Mrs. Geller: Oh, we're having spaghetti! That's... easy.

Monica: I know this is going to sound unbelievably selfish, but, were you planning on bringing up the whole baby/lesbian thing? Because I think it might take some of the heat off me.

美音小贴士：

- Ludwin 发音：/ˈlʌdwɪn/。

- They all had a thing for him. 妈妈很喜欢 Ross，为了表现自己对儿子的喜爱，这句话重读了 all，并且把 all 的发音拖长了。

- I don't have a restaurant, I work in a restaurant. 这句话中要格外重读 have 和 work 这两个词，用于回怼妈妈说的 "I told her you had a restaurant"。

- Well, they don't have to know that. 妈妈说这句明显是在吐槽，所以说的语速比较慢，一词一顿的感觉，尤其突出了 they don't 的读音。另外这里的 to 也无需弱读。

- I know this is going to sound unbelievably selfish...

这里 Monica 明显承受不住"火力"了，希望老哥 Ross 能帮助自己分担父母的注意力，所以尤其重读 unbelievably selfish 这里。

- 整体而言，老妈说话语速较慢，弱读较少，语调起伏非常明显，仔细听来每句话都像是在吐槽 Monica。

第二段（选自《绝望的主妇》第一季第二集）（旁白）

《绝望的主妇》这部美剧，每一集中都会有几段已故的主妇 Mary Alice 的旁白，这些旁白的语言用词之美，结构之巧妙，熊叔恨不得把所有的旁白都背下来。下面，我们来体验一段。

如果大家有兴趣，也可以关注微信公众号"熊叔英语"，回复"绝望的主妇"，获取更多的旁白精讲和跟读训练。

Life was suddenly full of possibilities. Not to mention a few unexpected surprises.

生命突然充满了无限的可能，更有一些意料之外的惊喜。

An odd thing happens when we die. Taste, touch, smell, and sound become a distant memory. But our sight—ah, our sight expands, and we can suddenly see the world we've left behind so clearly. Of course, most of what's visible to the dead could also be seen by the living, if they'd only take the time to look.

人死后会有奇怪的事发生。味觉、触觉、嗅觉和听觉都成为遥远的回忆，但视觉却变开阔了，突然能把身后的这个世界看得如此清楚。当然，大多数死人能看见的世界，活着的人也能看清楚，只要他们愿意花时间去看。

美音小贴士：

模仿诉说《绝望的主妇》中的旁白时，感情一定要丰富，说的每句话都像是对人生的终极感悟。这些旁白语速相对偏慢，停顿较多，重读和拖长的音也较多，抑扬顿挫很丰富，感情很细腻。比如前两句：

Life ~/ was suddenly / full of possibilities. Not to mention~/ a few~ unexpected surprises.

这两句中出现了很多停顿和拖长的发音。把节奏放缓，才更方便于表达细腻的情感。

第三段（选自《摩登家庭》第一季第 24 集）

《摩登家庭》是一部非常有趣、温馨的都市喜剧，伪纪录片的模式，也让这部剧充满了特色。这部剧最厉害的地方在于，它超越了普通的搞笑情景的设定，观众往往笑着笑着就被感动到了。

这里选取的内容是一大家人准备拍全家福的情节。Claire 来负责组织这件事儿。Claire 和 Phil 是一对情侣，Phil 给人的感觉经常是有点童心未泯，有些时候会沉浸在自己的世界里。所以当 Claire 要求 Phil 重视这次全家福的拍摄时，发生了下面这段对话：

Claire: Oh, honey, have a great time at the game!

Claire: 哦，亲爱的，好好享受比赛！

Phil: Thanks.

Phil: 谢谢。

Claire: Mwa! Why are you... crunching?

Claire: Mwa！你身上为什么……在响？

Phil: Ordinarily, I'm a rule follower, but when someone tells me I can't bring my own snacks into their stadium, that's when I get a little nuts. It's a free country, right? Let's just say it ruffles me. ...when some goobers...tell me I have to spend half my payday...on their hot dogs.

Phil: 一般来讲，我是会遵守规矩的，但当有人跟我说我不能带着自己的零食进入他们的体育馆时，我会有点抓狂（nuts 也有坚果的意思）。这个国家是自由的，对吧？让我不高兴（ruffle 也有薯片的意思）的是，有些傻子（goobers 也可以是花生）跟我说我需要把时间花在他们的热狗上，我可是牺牲了今天一半的工钱来的啊。

Claire: Please, just remember the family portrait. We only have the photographer for an hour.

Claire: 请一定要记住我们的全家福照片。那个摄影师为我们服务的时间只有一小时。

Phil: Okay.

Phil: 好的。

Claire: Okay. And, sweetie, did you have a chance to try on the white pants I put in your closet?

Claire: 好的。亲爱的，你要不要找个机会试试我放在你橱柜里的那条白裤子？

Phil: Oh, what do they look like?

Phil: 哦，那裤子长什么样儿？

Claire: Is there really a more clear way to describe white pants? Sweetie, if they don't fit you, you're gonna be the only one not wearing white, and then you're gonna stand out like "where's Waldo".

Claire: 还有什么词能更清楚地描述白裤子吗？亲爱的，如果裤子不合身，你就成为唯一一个不穿白色裤子的人，然后你就会很突出，像"沃尔德在哪儿"一样。

Phil: Actually, "where's Waldo" doesn't stand out. He's super hard to find. That's the challenge.

Phil: 实际上，"沃尔德在哪儿"并不是因为他突出。其实他很难被发现。这正是挑战所在。

Claire: This portrait is incredibly important to me.

Claire: 这个全家福对我来说无比重要。

Phil: Also, his name is just Waldo. Sorry.

Phil: 还有，他的名字就是"沃尔德"。不好意思。

Claire: I spent weeks trying to find a time that works for everybody and finding the right photographer. So, if you could just promise me that you'll cooperate, okay?

Claire: 就为了找大家都方便的时间和一个合适的摄影师，我花了好几周的时间。所以，你就答应我你会好好配合的，好吗？

Phil: I promise.

Phil: 我答应你。

Claire: Okay.

Claire: 好的。

Phil: This is amazing that you're doing this.

Phil: 你做这事儿真的是太棒了。

Claire: Mm, thank you.

Claire: 嗯，谢谢你。

Phil: You're wonderful.

Phil: 你真好。

Claire: Thank you.

Claire: 谢谢你。

Phil: Get in here.

Phil: 过来过来。

Claire: Okay.

Claire: 好的。

美音小贴士：

　　《摩登家庭》中对话的节奏很快，难度比《老友记》大。《老友记》会有背景的笑声帮你缓冲一下理解的节奏，但是《摩登家庭》没有任何缓冲。有一位同学跟我说每一集《摩登家庭》她都需要看很多遍，才能明白里面的笑点。大家不妨尝试一下，挑战模仿难度较高的《摩登家庭》。

　　• Ordinarily, I'm a rule follower, but when someone tells me I can't bring my own snacks into… 原本画面是两个人在逗趣，这里突然切换到 Phil 对着镜头"接受采访"，这就是《摩登家庭》伪纪录片模式的一大特色。注意，平时生活中的对话和在"接受采访"时说话的方式是有所区别的，"接受采访"时更淡定，停顿相对更多。

　　• Is there really a more clear way to describe white pants? 这里 Claire 已经有点烦燥了。如前面所说，Phil 习惯处在自己的世界里，所以对 Claire 说的话根本听不进去，所以说这句话时 Claire 有点受不了了，语速加快，语调上扬。当然，这句话也完全可以用降调来读，毕竟是 Claire 被逼急了说出来的，所以根本不是一个问题，而是一句吐槽。

　　• So, if you could just promise me that you'll cooperate, okay? Clarie 故作镇定地说出这句话，所以我们完全可以把 if you could just promise 这里重读，希望对方能重视起来。

　　• Get in here. Phil 习惯在说这种只有两、三个单词的短句时拖长最后一个单词的发音，显得很可爱。

◎ 自信演讲

　　演讲时语速往往较慢，停顿会很多，拖长发音的词很多，降调也会很多。大部分演讲中，排比句式会比较多，非常有激情或有说服力。下面的三段素材中，熊叔会帮大家直接把可以执行停顿的地方画出来（标点符号自动停顿），供大家模仿参考。

第一段（素材选自演员郑凯在综艺节目《奔跑吧兄弟》第六季中发表的英文演讲）

Ladies and gentlemen. Good evening.

女士们、先生们，大家晚上好。

Here / is a question for you. What would you do / with half bottle of water left?

请问各位，喝剩一半的瓶装水你会怎么处理？

Option A: throw it away. Option B: keep it / and drink later.

选项一：扔掉。选项二：留着以后喝。

That's nice. It seems / that all of you here today / is water resources activists.

很好。看来，今天在座的各位都是水资源卫士。

I'm really happy to see that. Well done !

我很高兴看到这样（的结果），真棒！

For example, let's have a look at this picture.

让我们举个例子，一起来看看这张照片。

According to the surveys, the total amount of bottled water / wasted in one day globally / can supply a million children / for three days / maybe even longer.

据不完全统计，全世界一天当中浪费的瓶装水就足够上百万儿童使用三天，甚至更久。

So clean water and sanitation / is the 6th goal on the 2030 sustainable development agenda.

因此，清洁饮水和卫生设施是（联合国）2030 年可持续发展议程中的六号发展目标。

China has a popular saying, " water and land, are our heritage / and ultimate wealth." It means that water and land / are our heritage and ultimate wealth.

中国人常说"绿水青山就是金山银山"，意思为美好的环境是我们宝贵的财富。

So I believe, we can all make a difference / in this world, starting / with saving (half) bottle of water.

所以我相信，我们从节约半瓶水开始，每个人都能够给这个世界带来不同。

第二段（素材选自马丁·路德·金的演讲《我有一个梦想》）

这次演讲可以说是 20 世纪最伟大的演讲。强大的气势、巧妙的比喻、极致的现场情绪，在几十年后我们再来听，仍然是最佳的演讲！

I have a dream / that one day / this nation will rise up / and live out the true meaning of its creed, "We hold these truths / to be self-evident, that all~ men / are created equal."

我梦想有一天，这个国家会站立起来，真正实现其信条的真谛："我们认为人人生而平等的真理不言而喻。"

I have a dream / that one day / on the red hills of Georgia, the sons of former slaves / and the sons of former slave owners / will be able to sit down together / at the table of brotherhood.

我梦想有一天，在佐治亚的红山上，昔日奴隶的后嗣将能够和奴隶主的后嗣坐在一起，共叙兄弟情谊。

I have a dream / that one day / even the state of Mississippi, a state / sweltering with the heat of injustice, sweltering / with the heat of oppression, will be transformed / into an oasis of freedom / and justice.

我梦想有一天，甚至连密西西比州这个正义匿迹、压迫成风，如同沙漠般的地方，也将变成绿洲，充满自由和正义。

I have a dream / that my four little children / will one day live in a nation / where they will not be judged by the color of their skin/ but by the content of their character.

我梦想有一天，我的四个孩子将生活在一个不是以他们的肤色，而是以他们的品格优劣来评价他们的国度里。

I have a dream today!

今天，我有一个梦想。

I have a dream / that one day, down in Alabama, with its vicious racists, with its governor / having his lips / dripping with the words of "interposition" and "nullification"　— one day / right there in Alabama / little black boys and black girls / will be able to join hands / with little white boys and white girls as sisters and brothers.

我梦想有一天，亚拉巴马州能够有所转变，尽管该州州长现在仍然满口异议，反对联邦法令，但有朝一日，那里的黑人男孩和女孩将能与白人男孩和女孩情同骨肉，携手并立。

I have a dream today!

今天，我有一个梦想。

第三段（选自杨澜的演讲《重塑中国的一代》）

杨澜的这篇演讲有种娓娓道来的感觉，可能不是那么激情，但是却很细腻。参考停顿如下：

My generation / has been very fortunate / to witness / and participate / in the historic transformation of China / that has made so many changes / in the past 20, 30 years. I remember that in the year of 1990, when I was graduating from college, I was applying for a job / in the sales department / of the first five-star hotel in Beijing, Great Wall Sheraton. It's still there. So, after being interrogated by this Japanese manager / for a half an hour, he finally said, "so, Miss Yang, do you have any questions to ask me?" I summoned my courage and poise / and said, "yes, but could you let me know, what actually do you sell?" I didn't have a clue / what a sales department was about / in a five-star hotel. That was the first day / I set my foot in a five-star hotel.

　　我这个年代的人是幸运的，我们目睹并参与了中国历史性的变化。在过去的二三十年里中国发生了很多变化。我还记得在1990 年的时候，我刚好大学毕业，当时申请了北京的一个五星级饭店的营销的工作。这个宾馆现在还存在，叫喜来登长城饭店。在被一位日本经理询问了半小时之后，他在面试要结束的时候说："杨小姐，你有问题要问我吗？"我鼓起了勇气，镇定地问："你能不能告诉我，你们是卖什么的？"因为我当时完全不知道一个五星级饭店的销售部要做什么。那是我第一次走进一家五星级饭店。

So, making a living is not that easy / for young people. College graduates are not in short supply. In urban areas, college graduates find / the starting salary / is about 400 US dollars a month, while the average rent / is above $500. So, what do they do? They have to share space — squeezed in very limited space / to save money — and they call themselves tribe of ants. And for those who are ready to get married / and buy their apartment, they figured out they have to work for 30 to 40 years / to afford their first apartment...

　　年轻一代人的日子不是那么好过。大学毕业生的供应超过需求。在城市里，大学毕业生的起薪大约是 400 美元一个月，但平均每月的房屋租金要超过 500 美元。那怎么办呢？他们只能一起挤在一个狭小的空间里，就为了省钱。他们称自己为蚁族。至于那些打算结婚还要买房的人，他们认识到自己要打 30 ~ 40 年的工才能买得起一套住房。

Miss Yang，这大实话说得熊叔我心好痛啊。

◎ 新闻播音

美音小贴士：

新闻播报往往铿锵有力，声音中透露着自信与坚决。大家在练习新闻素材的朗读时，不妨从 VOA Special English 慢速英语练起，然后再一点点把语速提上来。多模仿 VOA Special English，能让你对语调的感知上一个台阶，因为它的抑扬顿挫太明显了。而把 Special English 朗读英语的速度提上来，也就是正常的新闻播报了。

尽可能地放慢语速，去模仿素材中夸张的语调。注意停顿的地方、拖长发音的地方，有必要的话可以用标记法标记出来。你可以在"熊叔英语"微信公众号中回复"美音综合训练"，找到相应的音频，反复跟读模仿，并且把自己的声音录下来，与熊叔做对比。对比时，你的语音、语调等任何细节都要认真练习。

第一段（选自 VOA Special English: *Former US First Lady Barbara Bush Dies at 92*）

Barbara Bush died Tuesday at her home in Texas. She was 92 years old.

Her husband of 73 years, former United States President George H.W. Bush, was with her at the time.

Barbara Bush reportedly suffered from problems with her heart and lungs.

Just two days earlier, her family had announced that her health was getting worse and she had decided to stop receiving medical treatment.

芭芭拉·布什于星期二在她位于得克萨斯州的家中逝世了，享年 92 岁。

当时与她结婚 73 年的丈夫——前任美国总统乔治·赫伯特·沃克·布什正在她身边。

据报道，芭芭拉·布什的心脏和肺部都患有疾病。

就在两天前，她的家人称，她的健康状况正在恶化，并且她已经决定不再接受医学治疗。

Second in History

Barbara Pierce Bush was born in 1925 in New York. Her father published magazines for women. Her mother was active in community service.

Young Barbara Pierce was admitted as a student at Smith

College in Massachusetts. While there, she met George Herbert Walker Bush. They married in 1945.

She and George Bush went on to have six children. Their second child died of cancer at age three. Their oldest child, George Walker Bush, went on to become the 43rd president.

As such, Barbara Bush is one of two women in U.S. history to be both the wife and mother of a president. The other was Abigail Adams, who died 200 years ago, in 1818.

历史上的第二位

芭芭拉·布什于 1925 年在纽约出生。她父亲是从事女性杂志出版工作的。她母亲活跃于社区服务中。

芭芭拉·布什在年轻的时候被马萨诸塞州的史密斯大学录取。在校期间,她遇到了乔治·赫伯特·沃克·布什。他们于 1945 年完婚。

她和乔治·布什在婚后一共育有六个孩子。他们的次子在 3 岁的时候因癌症去世。他们的长子乔治·沃克·布什,后来成为第 43 任总统。

就这一点而言,芭芭拉·布什是美国历史上仅有的丈夫和孩子都成为总统的两位女性之一。另外一位是 Abigail Adams,在二百年前于 1818 年去世。

第二段（选自 VOA Special English: *Why We Take "Selfies"*）

Why do people take "selfies"?

为什么人们要自拍?

Researchers at Syracuse University in New York tried to answer that question. They came up with some surprising answers.

纽约锡拉库扎大学的研究员们尝试去回答这个问题。他们得到了一些惊人的答案。

People who post selfies and use editing software to make themselves look better show behavior connected to narcissism, the Syracuse researchers said.

锡拉库扎大学的研究员们说，那些喜欢晒自拍并且喜欢用图片编辑软件让自己的照片看上去更好看的人，表现出了自恋的行为。

Narcissists are people who think very highly of themselves, especially how they look. Ji Won Kim, a doctoral student at the university's S.I. Newhouse School of Public Communications, worked on the study. She said because social media can be superficial, it is a good place for people to "work towards satisfying their own vanity". By superficial, she means social media is mostly used by people to share unimportant information about their lives — not deeply personal issues.

自恋者是指那些对自己的评价甚高，对自己的长相尤其在意的人。Ji Won Kim，一位锡拉库扎大学公共通讯学院的博士生，投入了这项研究。她说，因为社交媒体可能会比较肤浅，是一个让人们能"尽力满足自己虚荣心"的地方。她说的"肤浅"是指，在社交媒体中，大部分人都是分享一些关于自己生活不重要的信息；没有深度的个人见解。

There are other reasons, besides narcissism, that people post selfies.

People who post group selfies show a need for popularity and a need to belong to a group, the Syracuse University research found.

Other findings from the study include: there are no major differences on how often men and women post selfies and how often they use editing software. But men who post selfies showed more of a need to be seen as popular than women who posted selfies.

除了自恋外，人们发自拍也有一些其他的原因。

锡拉库扎大学的研究发现，那些发集体自拍照的人所表现出的是让自己更受欢迎的需求，也是一种集体归属感的需求。

研究还发现：男性和女性在发自拍和使用编辑软件修图的频率上并没有多大的差别。但是比起爱发自拍的女性来说，爱发自拍的男性更希望自己受欢迎。

第三段（选自 VOA Standard English: *Earth Day 2018*）

本段是标准语速英语，语速较快。不过在熊叔的音频中，仍然提供了慢速版本供大家练习使用。

On April 22nd, more than 190 countries, including the United States, will celebrate Earth Day. It is a day to reflect on the impact humans have on the earth, and to demonstrate and reaffirm our support for environmental protection.

在 4 月 22 号这一天，包括美国在内的超过 190 个国家会庆祝"地球日"。在"地球日"这一天，人们反思自己给地球带来的影响，展现并重申我们对环境保护的支持。

The first Earth Day was planned as a Teach-in, a day to inform about environmental issues. Earth Day's founder, United States Senator Gaylord Nelson, an environmental activist who was outraged by the lack of political response to gross environmental degradation throughout the country, said that he was convinced that all we need to do to bring an overwhelming insistence of the new generation that we stem the tide of environmental disaster is to present the facts clearly and dramatically. Every university should set aside one day in the school year — the same day across the Nation — for the teach-in.

第一个"地球日"本来被计划做成一次宣讲会，在这一天宣讲环境问题。地球日的创始人是美国参议员 Gaylord Nelson，一位环境保护主义者，他因整个国家缺乏对整体环境恶化的政治响应而愤愤不平。他说，他确信应该让新一代的人们坚定信念遏制环境灾难的浪潮，而为了达到这个目的，我们所需要做的就是要把事实清楚地、戏剧性地呈现出来。每一所大学都应该在学年里留出一天——在全国范围内——为了这个宣讲。

His plan worked: over 20 million people turned up for

Senator Nelson's first Earth Day Teach-in on April 22, 1970. And from then on, the movement grew spontaneously, creating its own momentum with no central organization.

This year, the United States marks Earth Day by highlighting the need to curb the dramatic growth in the world's mismanaged waste and marine debris.

他的计划成功了：1970 年 4 月 22 日，超过 2000 万人参加了 Nelson 参议员发起的第一次"地球日"教育。从那时起，运动就自发地发展起来，形成了自己的势头，没有中央组织。

今年，美国强调了遏制全球垃圾和海洋垃圾急剧增长的必要性，标志着"地球日"的到来。

◎ 故事

（节选自《小王子》）

美音小贴士：

　　故事类的文章，是很多同学喜欢作为朗读练习的素材。现在网上有很多的自媒体英语主播喜欢朗读这类故事文章，但是有些自媒体主播会对这类题材的演绎有些误解。并不是所有的故事都适合压低声音故作深沉地朗读。故事本身可能是轻松的、欢快的、激情的、动感的、催泪的等，一味地压低声音把所有的故事都读出了悲伤的情绪，会给听者在理解故事内容上造成很大的偏差。

所以大家的语调、情感等一定要根据故事内容来决定。你在朗读故事前，一定要确保自己是能够理解故事所表达的内容的。在故事朗诵或有声读物的选取上，还是建议大家多听听原声或原著原配的有声书。

下面一段选自名著《小王子》，建议大家在朗读前一定要确保自己清楚书中所表达的内容，包括每个人物、每段对话的意义，然后再加入自己的理解和感悟。

"It is the time you have wasted for your rose that makes your rose so important."

"正因为你为你的玫瑰花费了时间，这才使你的玫瑰变得如此重要。"

The men where you live, raise five thousand roses in the same garden — and they do not find in it what they are looking for. And yet what they are looking for could be found in one single rose, or in a little water. But eyes are blind. One must look with the heart...

你所居住的星球上的人们，在同一座花园培育了五千朵玫瑰——却无法从中找到他们所要寻找的东西。但是，他们所寻找的，其实是可以从一朵玫瑰花或一滴水中找到的。然而眼睛往往是盲从的。人还是必须用心去看……

"If someone loves a flower, of which just one single blossom grows in all the millions and millions of stars, it is enough to make him happy just to look at the stars. He can say to himself, 'Somewhere, my flower is there…' But if the sheep eats the flower, in one moment all his stars will be darkened… And you think that is not important!"

"如果有人爱上了在这亿万颗星星中独一无二的一株花，当他看着这些星星的时候，这就足以使他感到幸福。他可以自言自语地说："我的那朵花就在其中的一颗星星上……"但是如果羊吃掉了这朵花，对他来说，好像所有的星星一下子全都熄灭了一样！这难道也不重要吗！"

"You are beautiful, but you are empty," he went on. "One could not die for you. To be sure, an ordinary passerby would think that my rose looked just like you— the rose that belongs to me. But in herself alone she is more important than all the hundreds of you other roses: because it is she that I have watered; because it is she that I have put under the glass globe; because it is she that I have sheltered behind the screen; because it is for her that I have killed the caterpillars (except the two or three that we saved to become butterflies); because it is she that I have listened to, when she grumbled, or boasted, or even sometimes when she said nothing. Because she is my rose."

"你们很美，但你们是空虚的。"小王子仍然在对她们说，"没有人能为你们去死。当然啦，我的那朵玫瑰花，一个普通的过路人以为她和你们一样。可是，她单独一朵就比你们全体更重要，因为她是我浇灌的。因为她是我放在花罩中的。因为她是我用屏风保护起来的。因为她身上的毛虫（除了留下两三只为了变蝴蝶之外）是我消灭的。因为我倾听过她的怨艾和自诩，甚至有时我聆听着她的沉默。因为她是我的玫瑰。"

"To me, you are still nothing more than a little boy who is just like a hundred thousand other little boys. And I have no need of you. And you, on your part, have no need of me. To you, I am nothing more than a fox like a hundred thousand other foxes. But if you tame me, then we shall need each other. To me, you will be unique in all the world. To you, I shall be unique in all the world…"

"对我来说，你还只是一个小男孩，就像其他千万个小男孩一样。我不需要你。你也同样用不着我。对你来说，我也不过是一只狐狸，和其他千万只狐狸一样。但是，如果你驯服了我，我们就互相不可缺少了。对我来说，你就是世界上唯一的了；我对你来说，也是世界上唯一的了。"

"It would have been better to come back at the same hour," said the fox. "If, for example, you come at four o'clock in the afternoon, then at three o'clock I shall begin to be happy. I shall feel happier and happier as the hour advances. At four o'clock, I shall already be worrying and jumping about. I shall show you how happy I am! But if you come at just any time, I shall never know at what hour my heart is to be ready to greet you… One must observe the proper rites…"

"最好还是在原来的那个时间来。"狐狸说道，"比如说，你下午四点钟来，那么从三点钟起，我就开始感到幸福。时间越临近，我就越感到幸福。到了四点钟的时候，我就会坐立不安；我要让你看看我有多幸福。但是，如果你随便什么时候来，我就不知道该在什么时候准备好我的心情……应当有一定的仪式。"

"You know— my flower… I am responsible for her. And she is so weak! She is so naive! She has four thorns, of no use at all, to protect herself against all the world…"

"你知道……我的花……我是要对她负责的！而且她又是那么弱小！她又是那么天真。她只有四根微不足道的刺保护自己，抵抗外敌……"

"The fact is that I did not know how to understand anything! I ought to have judged by deeds and not by words. She cast her fragrance and her radiance over me. I ought never to have run away from her… I ought to have guessed all the affection that lay behind her poor little stratagems. Flowers are so inconsistent! But I was too young to know how to love her…"

"事实是我那时什么也不懂！我应该根据她的行为，而不是根据她的话来判断她。她使我的生活芬芳多彩，我真不该离开她而跑出来。我本应该猜出在她那令人爱怜的花招后面所隐藏的温情。花是多么自相矛盾！但是我当时太年轻，还不懂得爱她。"

All men have the stars, but they are not the same things

for different people. For some, who are travelers, the stars are guides. For others they are no more than little lights in the sky. For others, who are scholars, they are problems. For my businessman they were wealth. But all these stars are silent. You — you alone — will have the stars as no one else has them…

每个人都有自己的星星，但其中的含义却因人而异。对那些旅途中的人而言，星星是向导；对其他人而言，它们只不过是天际中闪闪发光的小东西而已；对学者而言，星星则是一门待解的难题；对我的那位商人来说，它们就是财富。不过，星星本身是沉默的。你——只有你——了解这些星星与众不同的含义……

"Where are the men?" the little prince at last took up the conversation again, "It is a little lonely in the desert…"

"It is also lonely among men," the snake said.

"人在什么地方？"小王子终于又开了腔，"在沙漠上，真有点孤独……"

"到了有人的地方，也一样孤独。"蛇说。

◎ 诗歌散文

诗歌散文大部分适合用低沉的嗓音去吟诵。不过有些诗歌描述的是幸福、快乐的场面，也需要适当根据内容来改变自己的朗诵风格。读诗歌散文时，一定要格外注意停顿和语调的起伏，恰到好处的停顿和语调起伏，能给朗诵带来更丰富的表现力。另外，诗歌散文的节奏一般都比较舒缓，在模仿朗读时，尽可能地放松自己，边练习边脑补出作者所描述的画面来。

第一段（莎士比亚十四行诗：*Sonnet* 18）

Shall I compare thee to a Summer's day?

Thou art more lovely and more temperate;

Rough winds do shake the darling buds of May,

And Summer's lease hath all too short a date;

Sometime too hot the eye of heaven shines,

And often is his gold complexion dimmed;

And every fair from fair sometime declines,

By chance or nature's changing course untrimmed;

But thy eternal Summer shall not fade,

Nor lose possession of that fair thou owest;

Nor shall Death brag thou wanderest in his shade,

When in eternal lines to time thou growest;

So long as men can breathe, or eyes can see,

So long lives this, and this gives life to thee.

我怎么能够把你来比作夏天？

你不独比它可爱也比它温婉；

狂风把五月宠爱的嫩蕊摇撼，

夏天出赁的期限又未免太短；

天上的眼睛有时照得太酷烈，

他那炳耀的金颜又常遭掩蔽；

被机缘或无常的天道所摧折，

没有芳艳不终于凋残或销毁；

但你的长夏将永远不会凋落，

你的美艳亦不会受损；

或死神夸口你在他影里漂泊，

当你在不朽的诗里与时同长；

只要一天有人类或人有眼睛，

这诗将长在，并且赐给你生命。

第二段（*The Road Not Taken*，作者 Robert Frost）

Two roads diverged in a yellow wood,

And sorry I could not travel both.

And be one traveler, long I stood,

And looked down one as far as I could ,

To where it bent in the undergrowth.

黄色的树林里分出两条路，

可惜我不能同时去涉足。

我在那路口久久伫立，

我向着一条路极目望去，

直到它消失在丛林深处。

Then took the other, as just as fair,

And having perhaps the better claim,

Because it was grassy and wanted wear;

Though as for that the passing there

Had worn them really about the same,

我却选了另外一条路，

它荒草萋萋，十分幽寂，

显得更诱人、更美丽；

虽然在这两条小路上，

都很少留下行人的足迹，

And both that morning equally lay

In leaves no step had trodden black.

Oh, I kept the first for another day!

Yet knowing how way leads on to way,

I doubted if I should ever come back.

虽然那天清晨落叶满地，

两条路都未经脚印污染。

呵，留下一条路等改日再见！

但我知道路径延绵无尽头，

恐怕我难以再回返。

I shall be telling this with a sigh

Somewhere ages and ages hence:

Two roads diverged in a wood, and I —

I took the one less traveled by,

And that has made all the difference.

也许多少年后在某个地方，

我将轻声叹息把往事回顾，

一片树林里分出两条路：

而我选了人迹更少的一条，

从此决定了我一生的道路。

第三段（选自罗素的《吾生三愿》）

What I Have Lived for

我为何而生

Three passions, simple but overwhelmingly strong, have governed my life: the longing for love, the search of knowledge, and unbearable pity for the suffering of mankind. These passions, like great winds, have blown me hither and thither, in a wayward course, over a deep ocean of anguish, reaching to the very verge of despair.

我的一生被三种简单却又无比强烈的激情所控制：对爱的渴望，对知识的探索和对人类苦难难以抑制的怜悯。这些激情像狂风，任意把我吹向四方，掠过苦痛的大海，迫使我濒临绝望的边缘。

I have sought love, first, because it brings ecstasy—ecstasy so great that I would often have sacrificed all the rest of my life for a few hours of this joy. I have sought it, next, because it relieves loneliness—that terrible loneliness in which one shivering consciousness looks over the rim of the world into the cold unfathomable abyss. I have sought it, finally, because in the union of love I have seen, in a mystic miniature, the prefiguring vision of the heaven that saints and poets have imagined. This is what I sought, and though it might seem too good for human life, this is what—at last—I have found.

我寻求爱，首先因为它使我心为之着迷，这种难以名状的美妙迷醉使我愿意用余生去换取哪怕几个小时这样的幸福。我寻求爱，还因为它能缓解我心理上的孤独感，我感觉到心灵的战栗，仿佛站在世界的边缘，而面前是冰冷的、无底的死亡深渊。我寻求爱，因为在我所目睹的结合中，我仿佛看到了圣贤与诗人所向往的天堂之景。这就是我所寻找的，虽然对人的一生而言似乎有些遥不可及，但至少是我用尽一生所领悟到的。

第四段（选自朱自清的《匆匆》英译版）

If swallows go away, they will come back again. If willows wither, they will turn green again. If peach blossoms fade, they will flower again. But, tell me, you the wise, why should our days go by never to return?

燕子去了，有再来的时候；杨柳枯了，有再青的时候；桃花谢了，有再开的时候。但是，聪明的你告诉我，我们的日子为什么一去不复返呢？

Perhaps they have been stolen by someone. But who could it be and where could he hide them? Perhaps they have just run away by themselves. But where could they be at the present moment?

或许是有人偷了他们。但是谁呢？他又把他们藏在何处了呢？或许是他们自己逃走了。可是现在他们又到了哪里呢？

I don't know how many days I am entitled to altogether, but my quota of them is undoubtedly wearing away.

我不知道我总共有多少天时间，但我的时间额无疑是在减少了。

Counting up silently, I find that more than 8000 days have already slipped away through my fingers. Like a drop of water falling off a needle point into the ocean, my days are quietly dripping into the stream of time without leaving a trace. At the thought of this, sweat oozes from my forehead and tears trickle down my cheeks.

在默默地算着，八千多天已经从我手指间溜走；像针尖上一滴水滴在大海里，我的日子滴在时间流里，没有声音，也没有痕迹。我不禁头涔涔而泪潸潸了。

What is gone is gone, what is to come keeps coming. How swift is the transition in between!

去的尽管去了，来的尽管来着；来去的中间，又怎样地匆匆呢？

以上这四段诗歌散文，熊叔都提供了正常语速朗诵版和慢速版供大家模仿使用。另外，大家也可以尝试给自己的朗诵作品配上背景音乐，往往会有更佳的效果。

◎ 经典金曲

美音小贴士：

唱歌是非常有效的练习发音的办法。还记得我们在学 /nt/ 发音技巧的时候吗？就是通过一首英文歌 *Havana* 学会的。歌曲中的连读、弱读等发音技巧都会被放大，如果在练习过程中，遇到了很大的障碍，记得把语速放慢。每一段歌词，熊叔会提供慢速朗读版、常速朗读版、慢速清唱版三个版本供大家练习。

对于发音，歌曲素材的学习法和美剧、电影素材的学习法的步骤大体类似。

Step 1：找一首自己喜欢的歌曲，可以是流行歌曲、嘻哈歌曲、摇滚歌曲等。多听几遍，看看歌词，确认一下是否适合学习。有些歌曲的歌词不和谐的地方比较多，不太适合选作练习的素材。有些歌曲的歌词就是反复吟唱，信息量比较小，也不太适合选作练习的素材。比如：

Baby, baby, baby, oh

Baby, baby, baby, oh

Baby, baby, baby, oh

Thought you'd always be mine, mine.

可能就不太适合用来练习。

Step 2：反复听歌，对照歌词，重复我们学习美剧、电影素材发音的方法中的 Step 1 ～ 4，确保自己能练会歌词的发音。

Step 3：再次反复听歌，把重点放在旋律上。这时不要求大家能直接唱出来，但是你需要达到的是能够在没有音乐提示的情况下，把旋律哼出来。

Step 4：这次反复听歌，把重点放在节奏上。注意哪个单词或者哪个音节的重读落在了节拍上，尝试不跟着音乐，自己打节拍把歌词读下来，或者唱下来。如果做不到，就把节拍的速度放慢。

Step 5：这一次，有了前两步的基础，我们可以跟着歌曲一起唱了！跟着原唱，该连读的连读，该弱读的弱读，尽量把节奏跟上！如果原唱比较高，你可以降低音调去练习。

Step 6：熊叔强烈建议大家自己找到伴奏，然后跟着伴奏吟唱歌曲。

第一段（*As Long As You Love Me* — Backstreet Boys）

Although loneliness has always been a friend of mine

孤独一直是我的朋友

I'm leaving my life in your hands

自从你离开我的生活

People say I'm crazy and that I am blind

人们说我被感情冲昏了脑袋

Risking it all in a glance

竟转眼间赌上未来

How you got my blind is still a mystery

你怎会让我不顾一切还是个谜

I can't get you out of my head

我就是无法忘了你

Don't care what is written in your history

我不在乎你的过去

As long as you're here with me

只要你陪在我身边

I don't care who you are

我不在乎你是怎样的人

Where you're from

你从哪里来

What you did

你做过什么

As long as you love me

只要你爱我就好

Who you are

你是怎样的人

Where you're from

你从哪里来

Don't care what you did

我不在乎你做过什么

As long as you love me

只要你爱我就好

第二段（*Time* — MKJ & Morgan Freeman）

美音小贴士：

　　这一段歌词其实是从 Morgan Freeman 发表的演讲中截取出来的，被改编成了一段很有激情的音乐，被人称为"抽烟神曲"。在练习这段文字时，不妨先将其当作演讲词练习，然后再按照音乐的节奏去模仿。

　　Money is not evil by itself

　　钱本身无罪

Its just paper with perceived value to obtain other things we value in other ways

钱只是一张有感知价值的纸，用来获得其他的、我们所珍视的东西的一种方式

If not money — what is evil you may ask?

如果不是钱—你可能会问，什么是邪恶？

Evil is the unquenchable, obsessive and moral bending desire for more

邪恶是上瘾的、强迫性的、道德扭曲的欲望

Evil is the bottomless, soulless and obsessive-compulsive pursuit of some pot of gold

邪恶是对金钱无底线的、毫无灵魂的、强迫性的追求

At the end of some rainbow which doesn't exist

在一些根本不存在的彩虹的尽头

Evil is having a price tag for your heart and soul in exchange for financial success at any cost

邪恶是你内心不惜一切代价获取经济利益的价格标签

Evil is trying to buy happiness, again and again

邪恶是贪得无厌地索取幸福

until all of those fake, short lived mirages of emotions are gone

直到那些虚幻的蜃景消逝

◎ 嘻哈饶舌

美音小贴士：

　　rap 的难度不小，想挑战 rap 必须要对所有的发音技巧轻车熟路，练到像说汉语一样自然。大家可以尝试想象一下挑战汉语饶舌的难度，用外语来 rap 无疑要比母语 rap 的难度更高。

　　当然，这并不是说大家就应该放弃这部分的练习。其实在所有类型的练习素材中，rap 反倒是最能提高我们发音水平的素材。能完整学会一段 rap，那你的发音水平一定能得到很大的提高。rap 本身也有多种难度，还记得音标阶段熊叔原创的那些小 rap 吗？那些就非常简单。在正式的歌曲里，也可以找到简单的 rap，熊叔在这里给大家找了三种难度的 rap，供大家模仿练习。

　　在练习 rap 的时候，除连读外，额外要注意重读和弱读。重读有可能会根据节拍的点产生不同于正常对话的重读音节，而弱读则是无处不在，你永远无法想象一个 rapper 为了赶节奏会把一些不重要的词弱读成什么样子。

　　另外，一定要注意节奏。rap 不是顺口溜，要踩准节拍。每组 rap，熊叔都会为大家配上慢速朗读版、常速朗读版、讲解版、打节拍版、慢速 rap 版、常速 rap 版的示例，只要你有耐心，至少能学会前两个难度的版本！

简单版 (*Price Tag* — Jessie J，B.O.B)

Yeah, yeah.

Well, keep the price tag

好吧，留下那身价牌

And take the cash back

然后把钱拿回去

Just give me six strings and a half stack

只要给我一把吉他和一个扩音器

And you can, can keep the cars

你就可以得到我的车

Leave me the garage

把车库留给我

And all I..

而我呢……

Yes all I need are keys and guitars

是的，我需要的只是钥匙和吉他

And guess what, in 30 seconds I'm leaving to Mars

你猜怎么着，在 30 秒内我就要出发飞去火星

Yeah we're leaving across these undefeatable odds

是的，我们将不败的传奇打破

It's like this man, you can't put a price on the life

就是这样，老兄，你不能给人生标上价码

We do this for the love so we fight and sacrifice every night

我们为爱而活，所以我们每天都在奋斗和付出

So we aint gonna stumble and fall never

所以我们从不踌躇和沉沦

Waiting to see, I see a sign of defeat uh uh

等着看，我看见失败的标志（身价牌）

So we gonna keep everyone moving there feet

所以我们每个人都勇往直前

So bring back the beat and then everyone sing

然后回到那个节拍，大家一起唱

中等难度版（*Believe Me* — Fort Minor）

Yeah , I don't want to be the one to blame

我不想去责备

You like fun and games

你喜欢娱乐喜欢游戏

Keep playing, I'm just saying

继续你的游戏，我只是在说

Think back then we was like one of the same

想想从前，我们曾像是一个人

On the right track, but I was on the wrong train

在正确的轨道上，我却上错了火车

I like that, now you gotta face the pain

就是这样，你现在可以勇于面对痛苦

And the devil's got a fresh new place to play

魔鬼们也找到了新的地方玩耍

In your brain, like a maze you can never escape the rain

在你的脑海里，你永远也无法逃脱大雨，就像一个迷宫

Every damn day's the same shade of grey

每一天都笼罩着这样的阴霾

Ey, I used to have a little bit of a plan

嘿，以前我总是有一些小小的规划

Used to have a concept to where I stand

总是设想我会扮演的角色

But that concept slipped right out of my hands

但是那个想法从我手中溜走

Now, I don't even really know who I am

现在我甚至不知道自己是谁

Yo, what do I have to say

我还能说什么

Maybe I should do what I have to do to break free

也许我应该做我必须做的来打破自由

Whatever's happen to you

（以后）无论在你身上发生什么事

We'll see

我们将会明白

But it's not gonna happen to me

但是这永远不会发生在我身上

中高难度版 (*Love The Way You Lie* — Eminem, Rihanna)

You ever love somebody so much you can barely breathe when you're with 'em

你可曾那样深爱过一个人，当你们在一起时你几乎不能呼吸

You meet and neither one of you even know what hit 'em

你们就这样相遇，你们都来不及阻止自己

Got that warm fuzzy feeling, Yeah, them chills you used to get 'em

拥有了那样温暖又令人沉迷的感觉，是的就是那样的感觉，你曾经拥有过的美好的感觉

Now you're getting sick of looking at 'em

现在却连看他们一眼都觉得恶心

You swore you'd never hit 'em; never do nothing to hurt 'em

你曾发誓不再做出任何伤害他们的事情

Now you're in each other's face spewing venom in your words when you spit them

但是现在你们却换了副嘴脸，互相攻击，恶语相加

You push, pull each other's hair, scratch, claw, bit 'em

你们扯着对方的头发撕扯、抓咬、扭打成团

Throw 'em down, pin 'em

互相殴打、彼此折磨

So lost in the moments when you're in them

在那一刻你迷失了自我

It's the rage that took over, it controls you both

是怒火控制了你和我

So they say you're best to go your separate ways

因此他们说你最好与我分道扬镳

Guess that they don't know you 'cause today that was yesterday

想必他们并不知道是你造成了今天的局面

Yesterday is over, it's a different day

昨天已经过去，今天是不同的一天

Sound like broken records playing over

听起来就像是烂唱片放了一遍又一遍

But you promised her next time you show restraint

而你答应过她下次你会表现得克制

You don't get another chance

你得不到下一次的机会了

Life is no Nintendo game

生活可不是任天堂❶游戏

But you lied again

但你又撒了一次谎

Now you get to watch her leave out the window

---

❶ 任天堂：是一家全球知名的娱乐厂商，电子游戏业三巨头之一，现代电子游戏产业的开创者。

现在你只能眼睁睁地看着她消失在窗口

Guess that's why they call it window pane

想必这就是人们常说的"窗台之痛"的原因吧

9

最后的
一点嘱咐

利用好本书的素材，为自己制订训练计划。

在本书的开头，熊叔就给大家提供了一些练习方法，这些方法是贯穿整个口语发音练习环节的，所以要多多运用。而本书所讲的发音技巧，也是循序渐进，由易到难，从音标的基本发音，到连读，再到一些高级的发音技巧。我给大家的建议是：用 1 ~ 2 周的时间，先通读一遍全书，大致了解所有的发音技巧，然后用 2 ~ 3 个月的时间进行不间断的训练。注意，一定是不间断地训练，这意味着你不能前一天练习了 10 个小时，第二天就不练习了。生活中的零碎时间，都可以拿来做小型的口头训练。每天至少练习半个小时以上，周末可以多练习一些时间。

音标部分，熊叔建议大家用 3 周左右的时间练习。受方言影响严重的同学，一定要保持不间断的练习，否则你纠正过来的发音很容易忘掉。

连读部分，熊叔建议大家用 2 周左右的时间练习。其中，1 周的时间聚焦于连读的发音技巧上，另外 1 周的时间，用来回顾本书前半部分音标练习中出现的句子，看看其中是否有涉及的连读技巧。

本书后半部分的发音技巧，熊叔建议大家用 4 周的时间进行练习。同样，建议大家在学习的同时，也一边回顾前文内容出现的句子素材，看看是否有新的发音技巧可以应用。

在最后的综合练习中，希望大家能放慢脚步，如果可以，每种素材都要练习一周以上。同时，熊叔建议每个素材都先听 100 遍以上再开始练习。如果想让自己的发音更地道，建议大家跟着本书反反复复地听熊叔的声音。

　　还是要提醒大家，我们学英语，没有语言环境，这是天然的劣势，所以需要大家不间断地反复练习。同时大家要学会监督自己的练习成果，最简单的办法就是录下自己的发音，和熊叔做对比。

　　最后，希望熊叔在本书所讲的发音技巧能够帮助你把英语口语说得更地道，更接近美国人的发音。但是这也有一个前提，就是你的英语水平首先要到位。对于零基础的同学，你们不要急于一时，熊叔建议你们先学音标的部分，等英语水平有所提高了再进行后面发音技巧的学习。毕竟连句子都看不懂的时候，想地道地读出这个句子来，这本身就是揠苗助长。

　　跟着熊叔，练出一口地道美语，待到出国旅游时，一开口就让外国人把你当成 ABC（American-Born-Chinese）！